SUTTON COLDFIELD
IN THE FIFTIES

Part 1 – The Early Fifties

SUTTON COLDFIELD
IN THE FIFTIES

Part 1 – The Early Fifties

John Bassett

BREWIN BOOKS

First published by
Brewin Books Ltd, 56 Alcester Road,
Studley, Warwickshire B80 7LG in 2005

www.brewinbooks.com

ISBN 1 85858 229 6

A Cataloguing in Publication Record
for this title is available from the British Library.

Typeset in Times
Printed in Great Britain by
The Cromwell Press

CONTENTS

ACKNOWLEDGEMENTS

The author is grateful to all the many contributors to this book and the considerable specialist support from the Sutton Coldfield Library Local Studies Department and their Sutton Coldfield News archives.

The assistance and guidance of proofreaders, Gordon Hudson, Terry Bath and Alan Beebee is most appreciated.

Again the support and tolerance of my wife, has been essential to complete the MSS.

The Brewin Staff, have again been most supportive through their specialist skills.

INTRODUCTION

The original idea to cover some significant Sutton Coldfield local issues between 1945-1960 based on eight months systematic review of over 800 copies of the Sutton Coldfield News in the central Sutton Library, plus my own experiences of living in the town 1935-1963, seemed feasible in the planning stage.

It gradually became apparent from the considerable quality of eye witness and photographic material, so willingly provided, that the time span had to be extended to 1930s-1960.

Eventually I had to accept that the thirty years which covered so many local, regional, national and international issues needed, three titles: Sutton Coldfield in the Forties with a substantial lead in from the 1930s; Sutton Coldfield in the early fifties and a national railway tragedy; concluding with Sutton Coldfield in the late nineteen fifties, including a world event celebrated on home territory.

I am extremely grateful for the encouraging remarks and constructive criticism by readers of the first book in the series, that recorded the lives and deeds of many Suttonian's, and temporary residents, which otherwise would have been unavailable to later generations.

To conclude, other potential writers, considering putting down their own, family, or neighbours' memories of the town, can find support and encouragement from the Sutton Coldfield Local history Group, that meets weekly in the Central Sutton Coldfield Library.

Dedicated to our son Anthoney.

Chapter One

1951 – AT LAST – WELL STOCKED SHOPS

The first Sutton Coldfield News of 1951 recorded the heaviest snowfalls for four years. More than one hundred tons of salt and eight snowploughs were used to clear the roads. Amongst the one hundred and sixty postal staff were 60 B.V.G.S. and G.H.S. students.

485,000 letters were dealt with and a new record for parcel and packet mail was set during the week before Christmas. Postmaster, Mr. F. Taman, told the 'News' "A small amount of mail had to be dealt with by the Birmingham staff."

PROPERTY MARKET REVIEW

In 1950 the public became more selective and were not inclined to pay quite such high prices for the larger somewhat more old-fashioned types of houses. Small houses with possession valued around £2,500 remained comparatively static. The properties that were in demand and which continued to exceed supply were mainly country houses and agricultural premises. The New Year's Day figure for permanent dwellings provided in the Borough since the cessation of hostilities was 781 – far exceeding the number of houses built by Sutton Corporation between the two world wars. The total number of houses provided in the Borough since 1945 was 1,271 (presumably the private and council buildings added together).

The Council had virtually dealt with all housing cases of those without a home or having more than one child.

PARK THIEVES

Some Park thieves were tracked down after a diligent visitor saw two youths sawing down trees within Sutton Park. On a nearby lorry he saw a birch tree and he took down the number of the lorry and reported the incident. The Park authorities had given permission to a youth to collect dead wood – he was later charged with stealing a fir tree valued at one pound fifteen shillings. The youth was fined twenty pounds.

Incidentally, logs cut from the Park were sold by the Council for three shillings and six pence a bag at the Holland Road entrance to the Coles Lane playing fields.

At the same time, British Railways withdrew two weekday lunchtime train services on the Birmingham – Sutton Park – Walsall route to save coal.

PUBLIC ABUSE OF N.H.S.

C. G. Teall, Consultant Radiologist at the United Birmingham Hospitals, reported that there were three times more T.B. deaths than those killed on the roads. An influenza epidemic in the Borough meant that the Hospital Management Committee prevented relatives and friends from visiting Sutton Hospital patients. An exception was made for those who were dangerously ill.

A Maney group learnt from Dr. H. Arnott that, as patients did not have to pay for a consultation with their G.P., "They were abusing the N.H.S." He made the comparison with the beginning of the century when every person had to pay every time. The doctor stressed that, before the N.H.S., patients seldom visited their doctor "yet managed to keep in good health."

Business people in the town benefited from the resumption, after three years, of the 8p.m. weekday postal collection. A postman in a motor van collected mail from five locations in the town. The service had been withdrawn owing to a lack of manpower.

A fire at the back of Wyndley Café completely destroyed a wooden building which at one time had been used as a tearoom.

DEVELOPMENT OF B.R.M.

Councillor Alfred. B. Owen, Chairman of the British Racing Motor Car production Committee, spoke of the development of the B.R.M. car. There was no assistance from motor car manufacturers. In their view, "It did not assist the production of ordinary cars." Councillor Owen, who later in the year became the town's youngest ever Mayor at 43 years old, said, "Support came from the leading motor car component manufacturers. Two cars had been completed with a third nearing completion. Two more cars of a different type were being planned for 1952."

TOO MUCH RAIN

A number of Sutton area farmers spent some early weeks of 1951 clearing the ditches and waterways to allow the land to drain efficiently and prevent the ground from becoming waterlogged. Dairy farmer, Mr. R. Francis of Streetly, advised the News that "heavy falls of rain had made the ground very soft. We have moved the cattle into farm sheds."

Water in the Park had been an ongoing worry for Sutton Council for some time. A Councillor warned his colleagues that unless the required £2,000 for dredging the north-east end of Powell's Pool was found, it could drift into the same condition as Wyndley Pool. He urged, "In other words, they – the pools – would be finished unless a vast amount of money was spent on them."

A thousand strong audience at the first Annual Meeting of Sutton's Friends of the Park, held in St. Peter's Hall, Maney, heard a deploring of the ruin and neglect of Wyndley Pool. Perhaps the £2,000 spent on dredging one end of Powell's Pool should be used towards restoring Wyndley Pool. Amongst many other contentious subjects, it was alleged that decisions by the Sutton Coldfield Council were upsetting the balance of nature in the Park.

There was downright criticism for payments for the grazing of cattle in the Park, shooting of pigeons, and the poisoning of foxes. F.O.P. Chairman, Mr. K. Blacklock, recommended, "If the council will only, in the first instance, consult bodies and organisations in the town and then a good deal of anger and hot air will be avoided."

1951 POPULATION CENSUS

The Country's first population census for twenty years took place on Sunday, 8th April. A pre-census straw poll by the News revealed a 50% vote considering some of the questions to be too personal and an invasion of privacy. Tobacconist, Mr. Wright of 12, The Parade, said, "I believe that they want to know too much. Questions on names, ages and residence are all right, but they want to know your profession, education and personal details, e.g. the number of times a woman over fifty has been married. Where is it going to finish?" Mr. Wright continued, "Is there some ulterior motive behind it?"

Mr. Charles Mitford, a Jeweller at 17, High Street, was of the opinion, "The census is a waste of time, labour and money." Mr. L. Phillips is quoted that the questions "were too personal." However, a Midland 'Red' employee, Mr. D. Blythe, and Mrs. G. Derby of Wrekin Road were both supporters. Mrs. Derby stated, "There hasn't been a census for 20 years and this will bring things up-to-date. The statistics will be a great help to the country." Mr. R. E. Langley, Sutton's Registrar who was in charge of the task for Sutton, answered the News reporter, "Questions included the absolute minimum".

"They would not be used for checks on individuals", Mr. Langley promised. The Registrar later confirmed "42 enumerators collected 90% of the census schedules by Monday, 9th April. Apart for one or two stragglers, practically every census form in the Borough had been collected." Whatever the News straw poll indicated, Mr. Langley reported that there "had been every cooperation from the public. Many of them had been surprised by the simplicity of the questions after what they had been led to believe." The only difficulties reported by the enumerators were having to climb locked gates and to call as many as twelve times at one or two houses in the terrible weather on 9th April.

There were no 'deadline babies' in Sutton. The local maternity units confirmed that "the babies all arrived well before midnight."

LOCAL BLOOD DONORS

According to the News, the town's first two blood donor sessions resulted in 90 participants on 8th May and 64 two day's later. The local Red Cross Organisation carried out the sessions on behalf of the Birmingham Blood transfusion Service in the Methodist School.

Mary Harris, née Roberts, benefited from the reopened W.V.S. children's clothing exchange – one afternoon a week at St. Nicholas, Upper Clifton Road. "Mom used to wash, mend and iron my clothes and then exchange them for points towards other clothes. I had many 'new second hand' dresses or frocks from the exchange. At the annual Exchange Fête I had my first pony ride and there was a lovely big swing."

BASSETT'S POLE ACCIDENT BLACK SPOT

In the letters page M. Elyes of Canwell agreed with the recent support for a traffic roundabout at Bassett's Pole cross roads. The writer mentioned, "Many fatal accidents and countless minor ones had happened over the last 20 years. The resident knew that thousands of pounds had been spent before the war on improving the cross roads, but it had done no good." He pressed the authorities "to do something about the need for a roundabout, not Halt signs which did not eradicate the problems."

FESTIVAL OF BRITAIN FIRE

Holly Knoll was the site for Sutton's second contribution to the Festival of Britain fires. 21year old Philip Meade, assisted by other Sutton youth leaders, lit the fire.

The crowd around the blaze joined in community singing led by Mr. Simpson, the Youth Organiser. Accompanied by an accordion, the singing went on well into the night. Typical songs and melodies were 'Danny Boy', 'Polly Wolly Doodle', plus new ones like 'The song of the Festival Fires' which had been specially written by Harold Purcell.

The Sutton Coldfield Boy Scouts Festival of Britain Week closed with a gang show in Sutton Town Hall. Even the wet weather did not dampen the enthusiasm and high spirits of the scouts and cubs.

Dr. John Raine's copy of the green and white fronted Souvenir Booklet at 1/- lists the ten scout and cub activities from the Sunday April 29th including Scout's festival of Britain Service at the Express Cinema, conducted by The Revd. J. H. Boggon. At the conclusion of the service, Brig. E. A. James took the salute at the March Past on Sutton parade.

On three days the Orange grove ballroom was used, with a Scout Display on the Monday, a Cub Display on the Tuesday and an Old Scout's Re-union on Thursday. The Sea Scout's Display was proudly performed on Powell's pool on Wednesday. Saturday 5th May was busy. The Sports on the Girls' High School Playing fields, was followed by an 8.30p.m. Camp fire at Holly Knoll, led by Mr. Harry A. Hilton of the Yorks Wood Rovers. Ralph Reader's "We'll Live for Ever", a musical play of scouting in 1951, was performed on the 7th and 8th May. The production was by Robin Griffin and Russell Wood. Amongst the souvenir advertisers were: Betty Pitchford, No.1 Shop in Rectory Road, for Nylons, Hosiery, Drapery, Household linen etc. Scout Clothing was available from Eric Houghton, 35 Birmingham road and Stella Tyre Experts in Hill Village Road stocked car, commercial and agricultural tyres.

G.E.C. T.V. model BT2147 was £45. 3. 0d. Vesey Cordial Co. Ltd. Of Highbridge Road sold Crush and Cordial. J.W. Hicks were specialists for B.V.'s G.S. clothing, and Sutton Laundry Ltd. on the High Street mentioned in "Sutton Coldfield in the Forties" offered three-day dry cleaning.

Festival of Britain. Sutton Coldfield Boy Scout Association Souvenir booklet (Dr. J. Raines)

HEADLESS CYCLIST

Among my timid characteristics were the fear of traffic when cycling and going to work in the dark. The 6a.m. start on the Four Oaks Station early shift brought them together in the winter months. My cowardly method of getting to work in the dark meant leaving Ebrook Road with carriage cleaner Bill Clayton at 4.30a.m.. Forty five minutes before I needed to be there for six o-clock. Mr. Clayton and a Bill from Coles Lane were members of the Vauxhall carriage cleaning team. They booked on duty at Four Oaks, cleaning the train stock for services that began there, then after breakfast, travelled down to the Vauxhall dept. adjacent to the station, to finish their working day. Bill was a pleasant walking companion, probably enjoying some company on the wet and sometimes snowy mornings. He accepted my nervous disposition, encouraging me in my work, listening to my moans about the job. I found it fascinating finding out about his work and "finds" on the trains while cleaning.

One winter morning when I decided three quarters of an hour extra in bed was preferable to Bill's company, my morning walk, when I seldom met anyone had reached between Tamworth Road and Little Aston lane, when my attention became focused on a figure, cycling slowly on my side of the road. But without a

Old Veseyans R.F.C. 1950/51 side. They played not far from an early morning scare for the Author. (Mrs. Eileen Hawkins)

head. My natural instinct was to look at the Lichfield Road hedges and driveways of the large houses. The fear of what it was kept me watching, as the figure came up to me. Fortunately before I was about to run and scream as it passed, almost hidden in the neck of the navy-blue mackintosh I saw a man's face, as he desperately tried to keep dry in the driving wind and rain. On reflection, I gave him the benefit of the doubt that he was avoiding the rain, rather than scaring other morning road users, like me.

ANIMAL LEFT-OVERS

Probably due to the mornings when I was up early to walk with Bill Clayton, my need to kip down for an hour or so found me sloping off to the Signal Box for an unscheduled sleep, around 10a.m.. It is likely one or more of the signalmen, informed my foreman or gaffer Shallis of the unauthorised sleep pattern developing instead of my working. Consequently two tasks were given me by foreman Webb to find some stimulating, or at least different work to keep me awake on my morning shifts. The early nineteen fifties traffic on the railways continued to include moving Circus equipment and the staff with animals. It was a profitable source of income

B.R. jealously held onto against the growing road vehicles, able to convey small and large consignments, throughout the U.K. and abroad. Although the station masters were reluctant to 'loan' a member of staff to another location, the Sutton Coldfield L.N.W.R. line gaffers came up with an alternative way of easing the main station's workload. For instance, when the circus train was serviced. After breakfast one day, foreman Webb, gave me a long hand-brush, fire-bucket and large quantity of disinfectant. He opened the large vehicle at the dock which ran behind the signal box, giving access on both sides. Having opened the heavy sliding doors he told me, "to clean the vehicle out with the equipment and use plenty of hot water." As well as taking my breath away, the amount and size of elephant droppings and pools of urine, stopped my already hesitant steps into the wagon. It seemed to take me ages to get rid of the mammoth size and amount of animal cast-offs, but I did. A much cleaner vehicle joined its contemporaries ready for the Circus's next venue. In 1957 a train conveying world famous artists and animals brought them to the L.N.W.R. station at Sutton Coldfield. On that occasion working as a relief ticket collector at Sutton park for a week or so, fortunately my job description did not include disposing of animal left-overs.

OVER THE EDGE

It did not take long for Mr. Shallis and foremen Evans, Webb, Signalmen, etc. to realise Bassett was not domesticated, or a gardener, so it was not a surprise that the first class honours of best kept station for Four Oaks in 1949, saw the station completely ruled out of any rankings in 1950. 1951 did not look very promising, either. There was need for another, keep him busy, activity. Mr. Webb presented me with yet another brush, longer than the previous one and a piece of wood that was to be placed at the platform edge, plus a large bag of white powder, and fire bucket for water. Again white lining of platform edging was not covered in the Victoria Road Boys' School or Technical College curricula. Similar to elephant clear-out, no demonstration or illustrative instructions were provided. After a couple of days the platform edges were white lined. Various descriptions of my completed work included: "A dogs hind leg" and "Help for the engine drivers when the station lights are off. They can see where the sleepers are by the amount of white paint on them." Fortunately the quality of cleaning improved, but not to former Junior Porter Ron gardener's standard. There was some satisfaction gained from staff and passengers appreciative comments on the brasses etc. Further satisfaction was received in assisting people with their train enquiries. Most afternoons on the late turn, during my lunch from 3-4p.m., I enjoyed looking up railway routes and the times of services all over the U.K. from Birmingham New Street and Snow Hill.

THE TIN TAB

Freres in his weekly Columns in the News, referred to the Falcon Lodge Estate's development. He commented, "the redbrick houses are inhabited by folk from many parts who, because of their large families have been given coveted exchanges from their cramped abode in a single room, in other people's houses." He noted how "blooming the children are", in their more open clean air conditions

The mothers, Freres had seen were, "proud pushing the beautiful prams." Some of the mums had "Piled the babies into prams once a week," for the mile walk to the "Tin Tab" Mission hall in Coleshill Road, close to the bottom of Reddicap Hill, where our family lived before moving on to Jerome Road. The "Hall was put at their disposal for a Make-do-and-mend-class under the auspices of the Midland Adult School Union." With children occupied by toys, there was a few minutes silence, a hymn sung, and so to work, with the use of an old sewing machine. Then back up the steep Reddicap Hill to the Falcon lodge houses.

A tragic incident happened on Reddicap Hill a few years later that devastated a family and a class at a Sutton school.

Mr. McCormack informed me that he "was born in Sutton Coldfield. He moved before the war to Birmingham to get work." After six years in the R.A.F. he lived with his wife at her parents home in Castle Bromwich, their daughter was born in 1950. The McCormack's benefited from the inter authorities policy referred to by Feres, because of his Sutton birth. Mr. McCormack recalled, he with the family moved to "Sutton in 1951 and lived on Falcon Lodge".

Mr. McCormack found, "the council Houses were excellent, but shopping and public transport difficult until the estate was completed. The people were very helpful and friendly." In the estate's early days, "we had local business people bringing goods to our door before the shops were built." Some out-of-town mobile shops began muscling in on the regular's patch, much to the pioneers wrath.

Incidentally Mr. McCormack's father owned a fish and chip shop in the first world war where the Empress Cinema originally was. "Mother managed it while father did war service. The shop was frequented by soldiers stationed at Sutton Park."

Mr. Charles Abbott, Mr. Frank Cattell's bailiff, hay making on the Falcon lodge, prior to the housing development (John Abbott Collection)

SUTTON'S FESTIVAL OF BRITAIN DIARY

Prior to Sutton Coldfield's F.O.B. Diary events Councillor Alfred George Beech Owen, became Mayor. According to a proposer, though Mr. Owen was the town's youngest ever Mayor, he, "possesses the oldest head." The seven Festival events were held in the Borough's Town hall, starting with the Festival ball, music led by Harry Davidson, a famous B.B.C. Old-time dance band leader. There was a crackerjack revue, "Nuts in May," on Monday 28th and a broadcast Symphony Concert by the B.B.C. Midland Light Orchestra on the Tuesday. A selection of amateur films by the Cine Society were shown on the Wednesday, with an Operatic Concert by Emily Broughton Players and Sutton Coldfield Operatic Society on Thursday evening. Friday and Saturday evening highlighted the emerging talents of the town's younger citizens. 'The Yellow Jacket', play was performed on Friday by the Girls' High School, and the Festival's finale was a concert by Sutton's Youth organisations, on Saturday night.

The Town Hall activities were complemented by a week long society of Artists Spring Exhibition in the Sutton Central Library. In June, Hastilows "Tudor Rose" coaches ran a F.O.B. excursion to the South bank Exhibition, London, including admission at twenty three shillings and six pence. With a number of other railway people I went on the rail excursion from Sutton Coldfield at 9.43a.m. to London for the F.O.B., at sixteen shillings and sixpence return. I may have used a free pass. I was impressed by the exhibition, its size and variety of exhibits. Later in the month the Empress held a special film festival as their, "contribution to the Borough's Festival Efforts." The sixday programme showed, 'Cure for Love': 'The Courtney's of Curzon Street'; 'The Winslow Boy'; 'Scott of the Antarctic'; 'They were not Divided'; and 'The Red Shoes'. Presumably the Odeon with 'Lemon Drop Kid' and the Plaza with 'Wedding Bells', for the whole week, believed their presentations would be equally attractive as six films in that many days.

CARE FOR THE ELDERLY

Warwickshire County Council opened the former Deerwood Grange in Wentworth Road, Four Oaks, as a "home for persons, who by reason of age, infirmity or any other circumstances are in need of care and attention not otherwise available". The accommodation for twenty two old people, of both sexes, had fifteen in residence when opened.

FLORA AND BIRD OBSERVATIONS

Before 1951, a flora survey in Sutton Park, seventy five years ago catalogued five hundred and forty five different species of flowering plants identified by botanist,

James Bagnall. Mr. Bagnall described the park as, "the wildest and most beautiful spot in the Midlands and of interest to botanists as yielding some of our rarest plants." Two researchers in 1951 are quoted as saying' "It is probably still true to say that no other area of comparable size in Warwickshire has so many interesting plants."

Later in 1951 Mr. M. Childe, president of the Sutton Coldfield Natural History Society, considered that Sutton Park, "contains most species of British Birds." Of the two hundred prevailing throughout the British Isles, one hundred and twenty species was "the parks contribution. Of the one hundred and twenty, about "fifty five are resident, the park offers hospitality to twenty eight regular summer visitors, while the remaining thirty seven comprise the more rare members of the winged community."

INDUSTRIAL FIRE BRIGADES

Sutton Station Officer D. Whitton, reported that the policy of manning the Sutton Coldfield Fire Station with full time firemen, rather as a part-time station had not been successful in retaining sufficient trained personnel. They had been recruited, but the Industrial Fire Brigades paid their staff on average fifty shillings a week more, with less hours. It was no wonder for 50/- a week more, less hours and paid overtime, only two of the station's four machines were operational during each shift of duty. With multi-machine turn outs, Sutton and district businesses and households could be at risk.

A local butcher's regular customers suffered in certain emergency cases. Freres spotlighted a butcher who responded to twenty emergency meat cards of fun fair staff. "pitched in the locality of his shop." He had no warning of their visit, so no extra allocation of meat. The butcher had "a small shop in a substantial community." His small business had been able to offer the fair families the emergency allowances, though he had to penalize regular customers.

EQUAL PAY

An Area Organiser of the National Union of Tailors and Garment Workers informed a local club it was, "time for a definite rate of pay to be fixed for men and women doing the same job". Some members speaking with knowledge of local circumstances suggested, "equal pay might throw a number of women out of work." After further debate it was "generally agreed that the lead would have to be taken first by the Government."

A footwear manager said, "prices of shoes on an average had increased eleven shillings over the past six months, because of the increase in the cost of leather."

BOROUGH'S HEAD GARDENER

Mr. Thomas. J. Allen "first became interested in horticulture from an early age." Both his father and two grandfathers were keen gardeners, all three "Keeping floriferous home gardens and allotments." Young Tom helped his father on his allotment adjacent to Rectory Park. Later in life, Mr. Allen "was instrumental in reclaiming the site and making it part of Rectory Park, as few allotments were occupied and there were lots of ramshackle huts and glass houses which had to be cleared."

Tom was impressed at the age of 12, with Mr. J. W. Burke "who was an exceptionally fine horticulturist. He was a fantastic plants-man and propagator of plants." Mr. Burke rented the Broomfield nursery from Mr. F. Pyewell, in Hollyfield Road. Tom worked at the nursery at weekends and during school holidays, also helping with his landscape contracts.

Tom left Victoria Road Boys school at14, later completing several commercial courses. Office life did not appeal to him. Against his parents opposition he chose a career in horticulture, employed by Mr. Burke, "that gave me a wonderful grounding which has stood me in great stead all my working life." He served in the navy from 1941-46. After demob, already a Fellow of the Royal Horticultural Society, he completed a very intensive twelve months National Diploma in Horticulture at Wisley. There was "much burning of the midnight oil." The course included "Botany, mycology, entomology, soil science, plant propagation and identification." Returning to Sutton, he again joined Mr. Burke for a short while before his old friend, Jim Parker, the Park Forester contacted him on hearing "of my year at Wisley and asked if I would be interested in joining the Parks Dept as Head Gardener." He started in the spring of 1948, the current holder retired in the autumn.

FERN AND DECORATIVE PLANT DEVELOPMENT

The Oakhurst glasshouse was fully repaired, with a larger heated 80' x 20' glasshouse purchased, sited behind the Town Hall overlooking the Tudor Road Bowling Green. A development of growing pot plants for functions in the Town Hall was pursued in addition to the established collection of ferns, used for decorative purposes within the Town Hall.

No.1, Sutton Park Camp, from the Boldmere entrance was the free accommodation that Tom and his bride Blanche, were allocated when they married. It was previously the National Fire Service training centre. They had to "keep an eye open for vandalism, it was converted to temporary housing in 1951."

PHYSIOTHERAPY AT THE COTTAGE

Mrs. Blanche Allen had trained at the Queen Elizabeth hospital in Birmingham as a physiotherapist, later working at the General hospital in Steelhouse Lane. Mrs.

Allen wrote, "on my marriage I moved to Sutton and was employed at the Cottage hospital and at the Holland Street Clinic." She also assisted at the Victoria hospital, Lichfield, when they were without a physiotherapist.

Blanche found the Oakhurst Matron and her deputy "were very sceptical about" the weekly antenatal lessons to enable the mothers to relax during the birth of their children. Matron and deputy were later extremely interested to find out if Mrs. Allen would put theories into practice when she gave birth?

SUTTON PARK CYCLE RACING

The Oldbury and District Cycling Club were the first people to be granted permission to hold a cycle race within Sutton Park, necessitating the closure of the park to the public. According to Mr. Vaughan some of the helpers were in the park by 3.30a.m. to prepare for the start, two hours later. The mileage Mr. Vaughan thought was about 60 miles.

A public address system was used. The races were open to amateurs, with entrants coming from a wide area. Breakfast was available in the Park Café, enjoyed by marshals, helpers and other volunteers. The racing finished at 9a.m., in readiness for the park facilities becoming available to the general public.

The Sutton Park Cycle Races in Sutton park, organised by the Oldbury & District Cycling club had a mileage of about 60 miles. (R. E. Vaughan)

COUNCIL FUNDED FIREMAN LIFTS

A number of post war stories were related by Mrs. Joan Reynolds when she was Joan Ashby. There was the lovely smell of bread from Hornes Bakery in Queen Street and the Goffe's Tizer mineral water plant in Upper Holland Road. Dr. Raine's remembered Goffe's motto: NULLI SECUNDUS – second to none. Joan recalled queues for bread and cakes at Baine's and Riland Road floods, towards the Coleshill Road bridge. Joan's sister recalled "when she came from work, there would be workmen from the yard waiting by the bridge to give people a fireman's lift along the road."

Joan worked at Saxton's Printing works in Newhall Street, in a poky, very small building, with a stream behind it. Customers at the King's Arms, in Coleshill Road, were offered nylons sold from a big case by "Johnny, a Black fellow." A little old lady "came around on Sunday morning selling watercress at the door." Joan appeared to have a sweet tooth relating how she looked forward to Kunzle cakes sold in the little shop next to Gill's the Toy shop.

BOYS' SEWING LESSON

David Gumbley was in one of the three first year forms at B.V.G.S. in September 1951. There class of 32 boys was in the old buildings just off Lichfield Road. David related in the winter, "a coal or coke fired stove heated the room. Sometimes the stove filled the room with smoke." All the staff wore gowns and "though most were sympathetic a few seemed bent on frightening and repressing us." Perhaps that reaction from staff was not surprising when the little darlings "jammed a cabbage stalk into the exhaust pipe of a teachers' car." Mr. Gumbley informed me that in "one lesson a boy was sent to the Matron for needle and thread. The teacher spent the whole lesson sewing up a hole in his gown." David believes some of the masters may have come direct from war service into teaching. He continued, "Some certainly practised parade ground discipline."

The music teacher had composed music for the school motto "which he sang most days as the Head entered the hall and climbed the steps onto the stage." When that was not sung, "we sang Kyrie eleison (Lord, have mercy) also to a school setting." David added, "In certain lessons we needed the 'mercy'."

The Gumbley family lived in a pre war semi-detached house in Heathfield Road, Four Oaks, built by Morgans, who had their office and workshop in Walsall Road. As Heathfield Road was unadopted at the time it had no road surface, that came eight years later.

GLEEFUL SCHOOLCHILDREN

Conductors on the Midland 'Red' Services including the 102 route had problems with the first ticket issuing machines. David spoke of the "conductor pressed the buttons to correspond with the fare and operated a slide mechanism to produce the ticket." The machine often stuck and there would be rolls of paper on the floor of the bus and a red faced conductor. Gleeful school children, including him were "unable to pay the 1½ d for the fare".

At the time when the number six Walsall Corporation bus started from Victoria Road, a number of times he missed the bus from the terminus "but was able to run up Mill Street and catch it at the top as it came along Coleshill Street." David found the Walsall service was reliable and only stopped running in the fog. "On the top deck it was always very smoky. On the backs of the seats were small oblongs of abrasive metal for smokers to strike their matches."

QUALITY PAINTING AND DECORATING

Jerome Road residents provide an array of trades and professions, but mainly trades and limited skills employees. Over the years a Jerome Road family of painters and decorators moved their customer focus away from working and semi-working class clients to middle class and above.

Leonard Smith, raised in Princess Alice's Orphanage, started the business up the road from us in February 1951, with the eldest son Bernard, on leaving school, joined dad in the July. 'Bunny' as Bernard was known in the road, gradually encouraged his father to "aim for the top end of the P&D market." This policy made them aware that

When Bedford Road and adjacent green sites become sought after residential areas, Mr. Leonard Smith's high class Painting and decorating services were used and appreciated. (Dr. John Raines)

this selected clientele always had money for quality painting and decorating. Bunny over the 50 years the firm operated could remember only two clients failing to pay on completion of the contract. The quality of service offered and provided for individual rooms could cost several thousand pounds. Apparently the clients showed their satisfaction with the Smith families work when it became routine for the team to be booked up, seven months in advance. Bunny recalled that the majority of the families clients were exceptionally loyal over many years.

David Wilkin's record of Victoria Road girls Schools only mixed class. There was only one girl in the class of Miss Ashton. David is second from the right, in the middle row. (D. Wilkins)

One of Leonard's younger sons, Clive also worked for him for a while. Roland Tillesley remained with the family firm for some time. Bunny was pleased that Suttonians in the higher classes of the borough used the Smith family skills. Bernard was aware the family business enabled him to enjoy a higher quality of life than Jerome Road residents could usually expect.

MIDLAND 'RED' EMPLOYEE

Back in the fifties, down the higher number end of the road, David Wilkins father, was a cashier at the Upper Holland Road Midland 'Red' Garage Office, where he received the conductors' cash and banked it. When Dad was on the Sunday afternoon shift, David "called for him, on his way home from the Duke Street Chapel Sunday School." There was always an annual Christmas Party for Midland 'Red' employees' children held at the Town Hall. "There was lots of Red carpet …. Always the same conjuror …. And Father Christmas."

ARCHBISHOP'S BLESSING

The flying of the Papal flag at one end of the foundation trenches of the new sixteen thousand, eight hundred pound church which will be on Jockey Road, marked an impressive stone laying and foundation blessing by Rt. Revd. J. Matherson, the fifth Archbishop of the Roman Catholic province of Birmingham. It was a ceremony not frequently performed. The Archbishop reminded the gathering "that it was a great occasion in the life of the parish and in the life of us all." It was the start of the "building of a new home for our Divine Lord." A memorable day in the history of St. Nicholas's Church.

COMPARING PUBLIC TRANSPORT
Neville Upton of Mere Green Road comparing bus and train services into and out of the city, wrote, "No train took longer than the nominal thirty six minutes to Sutton by bus" he pointed out the "5.15p.m. New Street semi-fast took thirteen minutes to Wylde Green, it's first stop". Mr. Upton often used the 5.26p.m. all stations to Lichfield, or 5.40p.m. all stations to Four Oaks, The 6p.m. referred to by another News reader, had very few vacant seats when he used it. He twice had to stand as far as Wylde Green.

Mr. Upton also spoke of the 5.35p.m. all stations to Walsall via Sutton Park as a useful commuter service and quicker than the peak-hours buses. In Mr. Upton's experience, "Birmingham City Transport Trams were largely responsible for the delay to main road bus services." In general trains could be crowded but "most are only comfortably full, and could easily accommodate any who care to gain a first-hand experience." He commented that a railway season ticket averaged about ½d per day for a six day week.

THRIVING YOUTH MOVEMENT
As mentioned before the Festival of Britain Diary of Sutton events finale was a concert by Sutton's Youth organisations. Mary Daniels informed me that in her opinion one of the Town's most important post-war features was the thriving youth movement within the town, leading to the Annual Youth Festival. "Every church in the town had a club and with the other youth movements like guides and scouts they competed in a friendly way in numerous categories." Such events "led to life long hobbies and friendships and a greater understanding of each others beliefs." Categories included: model and toy making, cake baking which many boys excelled in, painting, sculpture, poetry, essay writing, play writing and gardening. Winning entries were proudly displayed in the Gas Office, opposite the Cup at Maney. Mary recalled, "every club had a drama group, choir, plus many individual performers, both vocal and instrumental." Packed houses enjoyed the variety of entries, followed by a popular concert." Mary expected some of those certificates, "are still tucked away in memory boxes." Adjudicators included Mary Richards from Birmingham Repertory Theatre, well known musicians, actors, directors and journalists. Some of the spin-offs from the Youth Festivals were "people learned production, stage design, lighting and acting skills."

FORERUNNER OF SUTTON CARNIVAL

Years later singer's that took part in the Youth Festivals are in choirs and opera groups. Several graduated to become professional in their chosen field. In those teenage years a number "of the teenagers learned to love Polyphonic sacred music like Palestrina, and a vast range of traditional folk songs," the youth clubs of the time had fifteen to twenty one year olds, that could encourage lasting friendships and some marriages. Mary spoke of sopranos marrying tenors, and altos married to basses. She wondered if couples were brought together by different voice ranges?

The Youth Carnival, Mary remembered was the "forerunner of today's Sutton Carnival." Every youth club had a decorated lorry, going to great lengths to provide underwater scenes, historical tableaux, topical issues, all of which created a mile long procession, "raising a great deal of money for local charities." On occasions when a lorry was not available, imagination created among other things, "a great caterpillar with thirty youngsters carrying hoops inside it." On a hot day that was thirsty work over a long walk. Mary believed, "the festival coloured the whole year of the young of Sutton and created a pride in their town."

LACK OF FRIENDLY SPIRIT

A group of teenagers at a central Sutton Church astonished older members when they told them, "there was a lack of friendly spirit between the young and old of the church." Janice Moore remembered that the Congregational Church archives noted, "A special meeting was held between the deacons and some of the young people." The deaconite took the young people's comments to heart with Sunday evening services suitable for their age group and monthly social gathering after the evening worship for all ages. The church adults were further reminded that they, "needed a more welcoming attitude and were warned against dividing the church into sections." Another significant move, "was the introduction of junior church membership. Classes were started to train young people towards adult membership."

Contributor David Myers, gave me the impression there was a lack of friendly spirit from some at his church. He wrote that his cleric Head-teacher was a "strict Disciplinarian and a one hundred a day smoker." One fiery teacher was once boldly asked by a fellow pupil of David, "Don't you ever smile?" If a child was injured in the playground they reported for a two-fold treatment." The Head administered First Aid. But before the summary caning for falling over was administered."

STREAM OF PLEASURE

Dr. John Raines remembers from his young days a feature that has disappeared from Rectory Park, "The stream which used to flow for a distance of approximately one hundred and fifty yards along the south-west boundary of the park at the back of the

Corporation depot. I recall that this provided many hours of pleasure for the children of my generation." In later years it was diverted underground in connection with the Riland Road flood relief works.

John considered, "A particularly attractive feature of the park used to be the thatched pavilion of Sutton Coldfield Cricket Club." Thinking of 1951 and later he, "especially remembered first Norman Sharp and later Pat Bowerbank, who were both mighty hitters of the ball." In 1951, John took a picture of the land on the west side of Bedford Road. "As far as the Bishop Vesey's Grammar School playing fields, they belonged to School farm. That was a mixed farm with a small Ayrshire dairy herd, also growing wheat and root crops such as Turnips and Swedes. The fields and hedge rows have long since disappeared."

NEW SUTTON CLUB-ROOM
The staff of the growing Midland 'Red' Sutton Coldfield garage, had their own Club Room opened in the summer by the company's General Manager. The facilities offered included: two billiard tables and refreshment area. David Jenkins spoke of the local sports-social committee, "as a hard working lot in doing duties in their own time. Two dances a year were held in the Sutton Town Hall, with three hundred and fifty to four hundred attending. Council Officials and councillors attended." Any profit was to the Spastic Society. "Vera Lynn attended once to accept the cheque on behalf of the charity." Mrs. Maggie Bennett said her father, "Bob 'cracker' Burns was a founder member of the Midland 'Red' club off South Parade." Mr. Burns began as a 'Red' employee when the garage opened in 1934.

CLIFTON ROAD APPARITION
Sutton Miniature Railway driver Jim Glover had a white as a sheet face, when he returned with a late into the dusk service on an end-of-summer Saturday evening. Not surprisingly it had John Tidmarsh asking what had caused his colleagues ill looking face. In a frightened tone, Jim recounted seeing, "a pale shape flitting among the trees at the side of the track." As Jim felt the need for support and reassurance John accepted the urgent request to, "jump on the tender and come round with me next time." John explains, "Part of the track was quite low lying, and in the mist of early evening, we kept our eyes wide open, Sure enough, a shadowy figure all in white was standing beside the tracks." On pulling up, the, "apparition materialised into a lad, nine or ten years old, in his long nightie." It turned out that he lived in Clifton Road in a house which backed onto the line, and he'd just come back from his holidays. He heard "the train and had climbed out of his bedroom window to come and see it." Children on the S.M.R. line were not uncommon, and visitor's foolish acts that could have resulted in people being

injured. In another episode of Jim Glover's driving days, "on being given the 'right away', he set out." He noted how well the engine was pulling. As he approached the terminus at the end of the run, he was startled to see a two-coach train still sitting at the platform, full of passengers." Looking round at his train it consisted of only one third of the stock. John explained, "some wag sitting in the rear seats of the front coach, awaiting departure, quietly leaned back and uncoupled the coach from the rest of the train." The coaches at "a later stage had their end partitions blanked-off."

SURPRISED FREE-RIDER

Mr. Bill Hunt, the son of owner Tom informed me that the staff ran security patrols, which enabled them to observe sections of the line from two vantage points. Sometimes John would hide in the observation car, catching youths trespassing, that could have led to accidents. Bill Hunt had observed a young person in the bushes, as he passed with the trains.

The weather was fine, so he ruled out the Clifton Road apparition. During the next circuit Bill remained vigilant, observing the young trespasser some distance ahead, almost completely hidden from view. The driver kept his focus on the line, deliberately not looking up at line side bushes. Giving a swift surreptitious look back over the train, to check it was there and passengers were safe, he drove on. Gradually he reduced speed as though taking a bend, arranging the controls to slow down and stop. Quickly jumped off, running the full length of the train. He apprehended a most surprised and startled lad. Having gained his composure the trespasser advised Bill, "that you can't touch me, because I am Tarzan Junior's son."

Tarzan Junior was an extremely strong and well built member of John Collins amusement park staff. The boy, the original Tarzan's grandson warned Bill his dad would deal with the S.M.R. driver, "in no small way." Even so the father was firmly advised about his son's foolish practice of hanging on the back of the trains, at up to fifteen miles per hour. On page 108, in 'Pat Collins-King of Showmen' by Freda Allen and Ned Williams, Uralia Press, 1991, the boy's formidable father is briefly named. The CRYSTAL PALACE, SUTTON PARK information is mainly found in pages 101-108, though its association with other Pat Collins ventures pop up in other places in the book. Tarzan is referred to towards the end of Crystal Palace's existence and the eventual closure of the site in the autumn of 1962. "In the row of rides behind the Dodgems, was the Dragon Scenic, gradually looking more and more (the worse for wear). It was operated by George Corbett, and later, George Sutton (Tarzan Junior). Three paragraphs later we learn that the train hanger-on was known as "another Young Tarzan."

In the book's who's who – part two, thumb nail sketches of George Henry Sutton and son George Sutton junior are provided on page 251. The description of junior gives another insight into the Amusement Park personnel. "'Young Tarzan', son, George, born in 1932, started working on the fair in his mid-teens, eventually becoming foreman on the Dodgems, managed by Walter Hobbs in the 1940's. Young tarzan was taught about electrics and machines by Johnny and Jimmy Ryan, and he together with Albert Martin had the sad task of burning remains of the Dragon Scenic at Sutton Park."

FARM MECHANISATION

A farmer wrote to me about the reduction of manual labour on farms. "The advent of hydraulics on tractors and power taken off shafts eventually did away with manual labour." The farmer thought, "this started in the 1950's and progressed, so where there were perhaps six or more workers on a medium sized farm, one man was sufficient." Another labour intensive job that has become completely mechanised "is muck carting. Previously hundreds of tons of muck (manure) were forked out of buildings and carted to the fields to be spread by hand with forks at about twenty tons to the acre on average." The contributor found such work was, "very good for the appetite."

RAILWAY JUNIOR CLERK'S PERSPECTIVE

The Four Oaks Junior clerk from April 1951 – June 1952 was Richard Coleman from Lichfield. His duties as he remembered were, "selling tickets, dealing with train enquiries, despatching parcels, entering parcels on a delivery sheet, making up cash to be banked, daily balance of accounts and three times a week compiling the Traffic Book, which was the summary of all transactions and the basis on which the monthly accounts were completed. There was always a rush to get the accounts away by the fifth of the following month."

VICINITY OF THE HEADLESS CYCLIST

It is refreshing in reading Richard's account of a Junior clerk's working experiences that he too, found it was not all plain railroading at Four oaks. I am not sure if Richard was aware a cycle sprinting investigation initiated for him by Station Master Shallis took him into the headless cyclist area, though in daylight. Richard tells the story: "At that time the National Insurance record was a card which had stamps stuck on each payday. It was the clerk's duty to get the stamps and stick them on each card." The Junior Clerk returned to the Station Master from the Mill Street Post Office having purchased N.I. Stamps. But the stamps were not in his pocket. Richard decided they must have blown out of the pocket. "I was immediately sent back by the S.M." In no uncertain terms Mr. Shallis warned young Coleman. "If I could not find them I would have to purchase more at my own expense."

Making his second trip along Lichfield Road, "luckily I was able to find them on the roadside near Tamworth Road." Many years later that seems very fortunate. Richard recalls, "of course at that time road traffic was very, very light." On the railway, "trains were steam hauled and only a two hour frequency off peak." Another railway cyclist was Tom Compton. As the, "Goods Porter, he cycled every day from his home in Kingstanding. He was responsible for checking wagons in and out. There was a very busy public weighbridge in the goods yard which was situated where the signal-box car park now is." Richard also remembered the "main traffic was coal. Two offices on site were Evesons and F.J. Hall. Miss Bishop ran Evesons and Mr. Gardener and Mrs. Dawson the larger office of F.J. Hall. Tom did all the weighbridge work. If wagons were in the yard for more than a certain time, demurrage was raised."

Four Oaks Station goods yard line up of: L to R, Station Master and Goods Agent, Mr. J. Shallis; Junior Clerk, Richard 'Dick' Coleman; Miss Bishop, Depot manager of Eveson's Coal Ltd; Tom Compton, Goods Clerk; and Fred Bell, Junior porter. (Richard Coleman)

FOREMAN RIVALRY

Writing about the two Four Oaks station foremen at Richard's time, they "were responsible for Booking tickets outside the Junior Clerk's turn of duty. They also acted as shunters for the daily freight 'tripper' trains and the busy upside sidings where coaches were stabled." Recording their individual transport, "Alf Webb came on a bicycle from Hollyfield Road and Bob Evans on a 'Bantam' motor cycle. Because of their early and late shifts the only times they met was on a Friday in collecting their pay." According to in the "know", Richard, the foremen, "were really friendly towards one another on Friday's, at paytime." Yet he observed, but apart from that brief time each week, "they schemed how to leave the goods yard in a way to create the most shunting movements for the other foreman," when he came on duty.

THE IN BETWEEN MAN

In addition to chasing up N.I. Stamp losing Junior Clerks, Richard noted the native of Bristol, Mr. Shallis, "was responsible for all operating matters between Blake Street (Butlers Lane opened in 1957) and Sutton Coldfield. He was also responsible for compiling wages and Salary lists from the time book. The main building was on the Lichfield side. He was also the Goods Agent." Mr. Coleman's description of one of the Station's well known Four Oaks area characters was Phil Boston. "My abiding memory of Phil was his bicycle. Really ancient and he never seemed to go faster than two miles an hour. On a shift he helped deal with trains in the morning peak, went home and returned to operate the signal box between the early and late turn shifts." His rugged red face was sometimes associated with his off duty pastimes.

There were many exciting encounters between the foremen and the porter-signalmen. They had known each other for some years, so were able to recount embarrassing episodes from each other's lives, when the argument needed such illustrations. Richard recalled signalman Dennis Cartmale lived in Whittington. Richard's visits to the signal box offered to produce more activity than mine, of falling asleep. He continues, "We used to go regularly up to the box and help ring out trains and set signals. I remember one day fooling about trying to keep the bay starter down by hanging on the counterweight whilst another member of staff tried to pull it on. The wire broke. We had to call out the Signal and Telegraph, but didn't get into trouble over it." Perhaps that showed the status difference between Junior Clerks and Junior Porters.

PIGEON RACING TRAINING

Considering the parcel traffic arrangements at Four Oaks station Richard said, "The lorry drivers came to deliver and collect parcels as Four Oaks had no motor vehicle. The major client for forwarding parcels was the Four Oaks Spraying Machine Co. When it was quiet at the station, the clerk went on the delivery/collection rounds for a ride." There was considerable traffic with pigeons on training flights. There was an extra 6d charged to return the empty basket. A pigeon fancier left a basket to be sent on to another station, for a training flight back to the Sutton Coldfield area. Fascinated by these potential competition winning pigeons, Richard opened the flap to have a look" at them. He was called away. "Coming back I saw one of the pigeons sitting on top of the basket. We were unable to catch it before it flew off." If Mr. Shallis had expected Richard to reimburse the railway for lost N.I., stamps, how much for a prize pigeon? Two days later, the day of reckoning took place. "The man called for his empty baskets. He told us his pigeon benefited from the training flight. It had won the race the next day."

SUTTON COLDFIELD LINE PERSONNEL
Mr. Coleman brought to mind some other railway staff on the L.N.W.R. route. "Mr. Beswick was the Station Master and Goods Agent for Shenstone and Blake Street. Both had a busy goods side, coal etc. Mr. McCarter, was Mr. Shallis's colleague at Sutton Coldfield, again for passenger and goods sides. The Station Master for Wylde Green and Chester Road was Laurie Wood." Richard knew those stations quite well as he "covered both stations as a relief clerk." Richard was impressed by the quality of the Chester Road Porters Room furnishings. "Chester Road had a wonderfully comfortable room for Winnie Hulls and Alf Dayman. It was just like our own living room with easy chairs etc." Remembering Fred Bell and myself as his Junior Porter colleagues at Four oaks, said "we were always obliged to them because they brought the coal for the office fire. At that time most offices had open fires and these always gave a cheerful look," to the room.

NEW WYLDE GREEN CHURCH ORGAN
A leading Church organist, David Willcocks, the organist of Worcester Cathedral gave an Organ Recital at the celebration of the Wylde Green Congregational Church's new organ. John Tidmarsh found it a moving experience. Mr. Willcocks "went on to become the Musical Director at Kings College, Cambridge. He was acclaimed as one of the world's leading choral conductors" John advised me.

ESTATE VANDALISM
The significant milestone of the formal handing over of the Royal Town's one thousandth permanent house since the war, number eleven Chadwick Road on the Falcon Lodge Estate, was almost marred by premeditated vandalism. A spokesman

A rare picture of Falcon Lodge, the home of Mr. Frank Cattell, the owner of the estate. Mrs. Smith, the Cattell housekeeper, is in the doorway. (John Abbott Collection)

of Henry Boot & Sons Ltd, Great Barr, told the News, "we were the contractors who built the one thousandth house. On the night before the official opening ceremony some of the windows were smashed and mud flung over the walls. New panes of glass had to be hurriedly fitted and the walls completely redecorated." Apparently they had not had so much damage at their Birmingham area sites. Mr. Butler said, "children play on the scaffolding and throw bricks down which have been placed ready for the bricklayers." The firm had, "lost a quantity of materials, lead, timber, and some electrical equipment has been stolen. Taps have been wrenched off and piping pulled from the walls. New locks and handles have even been taken from the doors."

Mayor Coun. A.G.B. Owen, the Lord Mayor of Birmingham Ald. R.C. Yates, and the Borough Surveyor Mr. T. Porter; took part in the opening, with Coun. W.E. Taylor, the Chairman of the Housing Committee, giving the key to the Lord Mayor.

The crowd learned that Coun. Owen had spent many hours during weekends on the estate noting suggested improvements from residents and these were then

Sutton Coldfield's youngest mayor, Coun. A.G.B. Owen at the handing over of the key to the thousandth post war house built in Sutton Coldfield. The mayoress Mrs. Owen looks on. (David Owen O.B.E.)

passed on to the committee. Coun. Taylor further spelt out the Council's vision for the estate. "We are trying to provide on this site, a self-contained community. There will be fifteen hundred houses with shops, community centres, churches, school, library." Up to the autumn of 1951, "seven hundred and eighty three houses have either been completed or are in the course of construction. We hope to build the other houses and shops in just over two years." It was noted Sutton Council "had concentrated on the Falcon Lodge Estate, though some houses had been provided in other parts of the Borough."

UNITED CHURCHES VISITATION PROGRAMME
In some way following the Mayor's lead to go out into the community to find out what the people of Falcon lodge wanted to improve their quality of living, the major Christian traditions in the Borough joined together for a United Churches visitation programme that aimed to visit all house-holds. The two stage outreach involved every authorised visitor calling at thirty houses to leave a letter of greeting from the mayor and local churches. The second stage, a week later by a visitor, required a personal visit to follow up the letter. The team of visitors came from Anglican,

Roman Catholic and non-conformist churches including Baptist, Congregational and Methodist Fellowships.

Baptist secretary John Edwards was thanked by Freres for data about the 1921 laid, Garden of Remembrance in front of Sutton Baptist church, "in token of God's gifts of birds, animals, etc."

Warwickshire county Fire Brigade recruiting campaign saw Arthur Wilkins joining in November, after finishing his spell in the forces. He was trained at the Birmingham Central Fire station, then allocated to the Sutton fire station. Nationally, November 1951, had the first Supermarket opened in Streatham, South London. Many local small shopkeepers were to feel the intensive heat of supermarket presence in the town.

RILAND-BEDFORD SCHOOL NOT YET COMPLETE

The girls section of the Riland-Bedford school building was not complete. The ministry-of-Education thought it would be "possible to accommodate more than two hundred children." Extensions to the school and the "R-B Boys' School (increased to three form entry) were included in the Education Committee's forecast of major requirements up to the end of 1956."

The Mayor's 1937 car was sold for four hundred and seventy pounds. The new mayoral car – a Rolls Phantom 3 was bought for two thousand, five hundred and twenty five pounds.

A forum was organised by The Friends of the Park to discuss the Streetly camp site which had been permanently requisitioned by the War Office. The reason for the requisitioning, "could not be made Public," Coun. Keyse said, "the Forum had not been organised to create a nuisance but gather all the information they could, and try and see how more help, intelligently, could be given in the Park situation."

Walmley Residents Association were critical of the condition of footpaths in various parts of the district and the use of raucous radio cars touring the streets during the Parliamentary election canvassing." The result itself was the first time it had been declared overnight, at 2.10.a.m. Sir. John Mellor's majority had increased since 1950.

Miss Ashton's class with Head Mistress, Miss Henry, on a Victorian Day. (David Wilkins)

SUTTON MATRON RETIRED

After sixteen years as matron of Sutton Coldfield Hospital, Miss E. Freeman retired. She arrived in the town from a similar position at Epping Hospital, Essex. Miss Freeman was leaving "for a well-earned rest in Durham." The News noted: 1936 New wing took place of some old cottages which were used as accommodation for the nursing staff, costing approx. six thousand pounds. 1937 new massage treatment, new X-ray apparatus and infra-red apparatus – total cost one thousand pounds. Dec 1942 Good Hope, Rectory road, residence of late Mr. Ramsay Winter purchased. Appeal to public, raised fifteen thousand pounds to purchase estate of about seventeen acres, adaptations and equipment. N.H.S. Act. 1946. Brought about many changes in the administration of the Sutton Coldfield Hospital.

WELL STOCKED SHOPS

The Sutton Coldfield News reported that the town's food shops had not presented such a variety and profusion of commodities and displays of poultry and meat carcases since pre-war days. For Christmas 1951, the reporter believed "the Christmas gift problem ought not to have been difficult to solve," from the greater selection in all the shops.

One Christmas memory I still have is a sad one. I was working on the upside platform to Birmingham, at Four Oaks. Down the path from Lichfield Road, walking with great difficulty was the resident railway surveyor, involved with the reinforcement and improvements of the A38 bridge by Nott Brodie over the railway. He swayed onto the railway lines, package in one hand and rabbit in the other. He stumbled, gained his balance, further stumbling, eventually reaching the other platform. To see a respectable, intelligent, competent railway member of staff, taken over by alcohol and putting his life and that of train crews and permanent way staff at risk, still remains with me, particularly at Christmas. John Platt from B.B.C. Radio WM, thought these five songs were top of the pops, for 1951: 'Mocking Bird Hill', 'Come-On-A-My House', 'Too Young', 'Jezebel' and 'Cry'.

BOROUGH'S FIRST PUBLIC SQUARE DANCE.

In the last week of 1951, St. Peter's Hall, Maney, hosted the Borough's first public Square Dance. It was a great success despite an electricity breakdown. Not long after the 8p.m. start, further potential patrons were refused admission. With three hundred present it was, "rather more than the hall could comfortably hold."

Chapter Two

1952 – ROYAL DEATH – CORONATION PLANNING

HARD FUEL FOR HEATING

Alderman A. E. Terry was disappointed with the architects for the Sutton Coldfield Divisional Educational Executive! He criticised them "for still pursuing the hard fuel provision for the heating of new schools." To him he "considered it to be a most expensive method." Alderman J.W.Mayell responded "it was rather late in the day – a tender for heating having been accepted." Ald. Terry thought "that the best type of heating", he argued, "was oil."

The best way of alerting road users to pedestrian crossings was, apparently, to turn them into striped zebras, particularly in the vicinity of school entrances. Of the twelve sites, eight had already been 'striped' and the Education Executive had already received representations about the remaining four.

Paul, Mary and Ted Roberts lived in the first phase of building on the Falcon Lodge Estate, seen with the original plaque of 1949. A more recent tenant, Mr. Warner, keeps an eye on the 'youngsters'. (Mr. Mrs. Warner/Author)

Miss Badham advised the News that an intelligent chimpanzee, Susan, was learning to ride her own Shetland pony. Another step forward for animal independence!

FIVE HUNDRED PLUS FAMILIES ON F. L. E.

The Mayor, Councillor A. G. B. Owen, announced that "more than five hundred families were living on the Falcon Lodge Estate with further development proceeding rapidly." He launched an appeal to provide the estate with a church hall in a small brochure entitled 'Wanted, a Church Hall'. The Mayor was of the opinion "there is no centre for church life and, with this fast growing community, the need becomes more urgent every week." Coun. Owen emphasised "It is for the children that the need is felt most of all, for they have no Sunday School nor other religious associations necessary for their training in the ways of Christian life." Letters column contributor, Mr. A. V. Dwyer, wrote that the national press had identified that "Sutton Coldfield could boast several millionaires, even multi-millionaires, of both sexes."

The letter writer suggested "with great respect, it was a splendid opportunity to make a very nice gesture by one of the millionaires or multi-millionaires subscribing the whole amount." Freres "Wondered what would happen." The paper, over the years, wrote of Coun. Owen's, and some of his contemporaries', generous financial support of a number of worthy causes.

SPEEDING MAYOR

Probably a few Jerome Road residents chuckled in reading that the Mayor had been caught exceeding the speed limit in his Rolls-Bentley and had been fined five pounds by Walsall magistrates. Having been stopped when recorded as travelling at sixty miles per hour, he said "He had been driving through the fog at Sutton Coldfield and had been speeding a little." Councillor Owen added to the police officer "I am going to Scotland tomorrow." Some Jerome Road, Ebrook Road and Royal Road folk could confirm seeing him reaching such speeds with kids in the back – much to the youngsters' delight!

Crusader, John Tidmarsh, wrote that class members had heard of Coun. Owen's court appearance and pointed out that the following Sunday he took the senior group as usual and made a veiled reference to the incident in his talk – something like "Sometimes we all do things that we shouldn't and regret afterwards."

FALCON LODGE – EXCELLENT ACCOMMODATION

The Roberts family of 269 Springfield Road were accommodated in the first phase of the Falcon Lodge Estate, just up the road from the plaque stating "These houses, the first to be completed on the estate, were opened by His Worship the Mayor, Councillor Claud Dainty, J.P., on the 17th January, 1949." Mary Harris, the oldest of the three children, compared the amenities they had in central Sutton with the new Falcon Lodge development: "In 1949 we moved from 52 Duke Street, a small rented house costing 10s.6d. (ten and sixpence) a week. We had an old galvanised bath hanging up on the outside wall. The coalhouse, or coalhole, was in the kitchen next door to the larder with its cold slab. The toilet was an outside lavatory a little walk up the yard." Mary can "remember the black lead grate and the lovely rice puddings, cooked slowly in the oven. There was the toasting fork and the smell of slightly burnt toast." The Roberts family's first wireless came around 1946 or 1947 and they listened to 'Dick Barton, Special Agent'.

Mary gives a further insight into a working class family's removal: "A number of trips were made to the brand new house by foot and eight wheels – a large coach built pram, full and piled high with so many odds and ends, and a push chair, with two-year old Paul in. Dad pushed the pram, leaving the push chair to mom!" Ted and Mary carried more bags and packages. The family made the two-mile journey six or seven times fully laden up before "the open topped van came for the big stuff. The cat travelled in style in the metal meat-safe." Mrs. Harris thought her parents must have "been thrilled to bits with their new home. Outside there were gardens, a coalhouse, a shed and a loo all to ourselves. Upstairs there was a bathroom, loo, and three bedrooms. The ground floor had a kitchen – really lovely, a lounge, and a dining room – very posh!"

MISCHIEVOUS CHILDREN

In Mary's description of her and Ted playing on the developing estate, the contractors considered some of the children as vandals. "As children", she wrote, "we had such fun and excitement playing on the new sites." They had been warned not to go near the lime pits "because we could get a nasty burn." She recalled the new red bricks, lots of sand and trying to turn the handles of the cement mixers. Along with other children Ted and Mary "walked the planks – what a playground for us kids!" There were so many partly-built houses and "walking the unfinished roads and country lanes, getting covered in mud over the fields, visiting Langley Pool and enjoying the lovely bluebell woods – these were good days." Mary was told that the Black Prince had stayed on occasions at Langley Hill farm. After living in cramped city or town dwellings, for hundreds of children the Falcon Lodge estate and its environs with nearby open spaces became a wonderful place of discovery.

PARK LANE TRANSFER

Ernest Clifton was pleased to start work at Penns station and in the goods department in early 1952. He recalled the work: "I had to mop out the waiting rooms twice a day, collect tickets and help passengers." Down the road at the

Park Lane Transfer. Ernest Clifton's strained back in Penns goods yard led to signal box duties at Park lane Junction in early 1952 (Ernest Clifton Collection)

goods depot, Ernie "Had to handle 1- 1½ cwt. bags of Silcock's animal meal, sometimes putting the 1 cwt. plus bags on top of each other on a high shelf." Within a few days "I had strained my back." The Station Master, Danny Lander, and two signal inspectors gave him suitable training and established Ernie as a signalman at Park Lane Junction signal box at the Minworth end of the Sutton Park railway route. Ernie was frequently reminded of the Penns goods yard as he operated the release signal from Park Lane at Penns when the weekday daily tripper goods train needed access.

The four local permanent way gang. (Ernest Clifton Collection)

The two other Park Lane signalmen covering the three shifts were Peter Rayner and George Fern. Ernie also worked in co-operation with the local permanent way gang of Ganger Sid Dainty, Bill Wild, David Roberts and another Charlie.

A TRIFLING INCIDENT

In 1950-51 the Riland-Bedford School was not ready to take boys, so David Wilkins spent a year at Victoria Road Girls' School staffed by Miss Aston and Miss Henry amongst others. David then moved across Trinity Hill to Victoria Road Boys' School under its Headmaster, Mr. Gregory. Amongst the teachers was Mr. Rhead who was tall, thin, wore glasses and had an R.A.F 'type' moustache. Mr. Carter read 'The 39 Steps', Mr. Barlow walked with a limp that David considered was "probably due to the war." Some of the plays he remembers included 'Helen of Troy', 'Tom Sawyer white-washing the fence' and 'The Nativity Play'. Further teachers were Miss Reece, Miss Howard, Mr. Elms and Mr. Henshaw.

School meals were delivered daily in large metal drums by green Warwickshire County Council vehicles. "One day a canister fell off the van and tumbled down Trinity Hill spraying trifle everywhere!" Food was kept hot in a long, heated, metal sideboard in the hall.

David enjoyed participating in plays. He also enjoyed family walks on Sundays through Sutton Park. Mrs. Alice Dillon of 110 Victoria Road encouraged the boy to play the piano – providing qualified tuition to the budding pianist. When pushed, Mr. Wilkins can still sing the 'A.B.C. Minors' Song! "It was 9d before 3 o'clock and, with continuous performances, you could be there until the National Anthem!" David preferred 'The Odeon' with its typical art-deco look. The curtains bore the masks of tragedy and the staircase was a huge picture. He still wonders if it is still there under subsequent alterations.

JEROME ROAD LIFE
In the 1950s traffic was still sparse and David said "We could play in our road without fear of being run over." The corner shops were Crockett's (basically grocery) and Cleveland's (greengrocers). David used to play with Bill Winfidale and Robert Greenhill, both neighbours in Jerome Road.

HOOLIGANS ON THE MARCH
Examples of adolescent, vandal behaviour on the Falcon Lodge Estate were not restricted to the new model development. Prowling hooligans had badly cut, and in certain cases severed, beech trees on the corner of Thornhill Road and Streetly Lane. Some public conveniences in that area had their liquid soap containers wrenched off the walls and stolen. In one case a washbasin had been completely pulled away from the wall. In Manor Road fencing and coping stones had been torn down. The finger of suspicion, according to the News, pointed at hooligans and 'young roughs' visiting a dance hall in Sutton Park on Saturdays. They went in the interval to the Cup Inn and, after a few drinks, returned for the second half via Manor Hill and Manor Road – ripping off house nameplates. Many wooden fence palings were torn down and abandoned across the pavements. When questioned about this behaviour, the Borough Surveyor, Mr. T. Porter, replied "Outbreaks of this type occur from time to time."

KING WITH THE HUMAN TOUCH
Sutton Coldfield, it was reported, was shocked to learn of the death of King George VIth on Wednesday, 5th February, 1952. The Corporation, with its mace draped in black, paid its silent tribute to the King and saluted the new Queen, Elizabeth II. On reflection, I did not show 'my silent tribute' to the deceased King as, with other

teenagers, I was indignant to find the cinema, probably The Empress, was closed as a mark of respect for the King and his family! Mary Harris remembered: "Gloom prevailed. The radio, or wireless as it was known in those days, played serious music and mournful dirges. The nation went into mourning and I was very upset, not so much about the death of the King, but because I could not go to the pictures with my boyfriend! All the picture houses had closed."

A picture in the Sutton Coldfield News of February 16th under the headline 'The King with the human touch' recorded the Mayor, Councillor A. G. B. Owen, on the Council house balcony "proclaiming to Suttonians the accession of Queen Elizabeth the Second." The Mayor, as Chairman of Dr. Barnardo's Homes, was often in contact with the Royal Family who were Patrons with Princess Margaret being the then President of the charity. The Mayor added: "Let us look ahead with determination that we, as members of this great nation, may play our part and give loyal homage to our Queen."

Council House Announcement. The Mayor, Coun. A. G. B. Owen, on the Council House balcony, announcing the proclamation on the accession of Queen Elizabeth ll. (Birmingham Library Services)

The weekend after the King's passing away, the congregations at all Sutton Coldfield's churches held memorial services for the late King and the Town, as a whole, audibly expressed its sorrow with the muffled peals of the parish church bells.

Later in the year, Sutton Coldfield Town council tentatively revealed that the Coronation celebrations would be June 1st, 1953.

LOCAL DAIRYMEN UNITE

Fears by four independent local dairymen that they would be forced under the control of large wholesale concerns galvanised them to form their own company. The Government order would prevent the smaller dairymen buying raw milk direct from farmers unless it was tuberculin tested. In order to retain some independence, Messrs. C. Bayliss, O. Eaton, T. Maryall and P. Woodward jointly invested £6,000 to buy a pasteurisation plant. The four entrepreneurs were "quite willing to help any other small business dairymen" to hold on to their independence by using the new plant.

BIRMINGHAM REDUCE GRAMMAR SCHOOL PLACES

Mr. E. E. Timms expressed the fears of many Boldmere Junior School parents that the decision by Birmingham to reduce the number of grammar school places allocated to Sutton Coldfield junior school children lessened the educational opportunities and options for a lot of youngsters. As President of the B.J.S. Parents Association, Mr. Timms said "Parents were naturally concerned about the position and we feel that the character of the district warrants a higher percentage of grammar school places."

Another news item in the same issue of the paper demonstrated that the neighbouring city gained from educational and career training opportunities within the royal town, referring to the annual report of the Sutton Coldfield Institute of Further Education, the full-time principal spoke of the new day release classes for shorthand and typing.

All the students were released by their employees. Mr. Timms may have been interested to learn, that of those on the recently introduced shorthand and typing course, "The majority were coming from the Birmingham area." 1,606 students had enrolled in all the Institute classes with 1,312 taking part in technical and commercial classes. Another 294 students benefited from the facilities in the art department.

APATHETIC SUTTON CITIZENS

In stark contrast to the Boldmere Junior School Parents Association's agitation for more grammar school places, the founder of the Friends of the Park described the majority of the local folk as apathetic towards Sutton Park. The Friends numbered nearly 3,000 members and was "the largest membership of any body in the

Midlands apart from national organisations" Mr. Blacklock advised Suttonians. "Piece by piece this Park of ours is being taken over. All sorts of government departments, that never existed before the War, are casting covetous eyes on Sutton Park." Perhaps recognising a national disease, he stressed "The citizens of Sutton Coldfield seem to be remarkably apathetic about their personal possessions. The Park was extremely important to the Town."

Sutton Council encouraged Falcon Lodge tenants to benefit from their own efforts by allocating 29 allotment plots to them. Fourteen garages were to be built on the estate in answer to tenant demand.

EMPIRE DAY: FOR OR AGAINST?

The Sutton News reporters discovered that the debating temperature in the Town was raised in 1952 by the ceremonial observance or not of Empire Day. Some saw the practice of the observance as an out-moded 'expression of patriotism' with a present day trend of 'pandering to nationalism'. The 'Rule Britannia' type of mind was not 'to be condoned'.

However, the News said that Empire Day was zealously safeguarded in our schools and, indeed, elsewhere, in honour of a group of united nations who remain loyal to an enlightened form of imperial government.

Fourteen-year-old Worcester Lane (Four Oaks) artist, Barry Smith, completed a caricature of the Mayor having already produced one for the previous Mayor, Rev. H. H. Keyse. Barry, having been encouraged by the reception of his caricatures, had begun further study at the Aston Commercial School.

F.C.S.F.

Rod Spooner was a member of the Friendship Circle of Showland Friends that met twice a year in the Crystal Palace Amusement Park Café. They discussed the "showmen's traction engines and organs which were still travelling, though getting less all the time." They also exchanged photographs of engines, rides, etc., and their leader was a Roman Catholic priest. Of the Amusement Park, Rod said, "There was a good flow of visitors including coach parties." He learnt from an older showman "that Pat Collins stored a lot of his older rides, etc., at Sutton." With sadness Mr. Spooner recalled, "When the site closed in 1962, a lot of these rides were burnt on site, so much of our fairground heritage was lost forever."

SUTTON AMUSEMENTS

The Brookland Speedway was on an oval track with an island in the centre. "The rubber-tyred cars were controlled by under-floor electricity." The steam yachts were two big boats with a stationery steam engine driving each one alternatively like a

Pat Collins Steam Yachts at Sutton Coldfield in 1952. (Rod Spooner)

giant swing. They were a novelty for the times, but would be tame now. The wooden Big Dipper was the big ride at Sutton – it later went to Battersea Park. The Jack and Jill slide was similar to the modern inflatable slides, but it was a more permanent structure with a hill in the middle.

Another 1950's memory for Rod Spooner was the switchback. "It had seen better days and was, alas, broken up at Sutton." The ride's organ did not play very well as it needed attention.

The tunes were all older ones such as marches, waltzes and music hall types. A F.C.S.F. member, George Cornfield, a Birmingham City Council road sweeper "used to put the music books through the key frame" continued Mr. Spooner.

BIG DIPPER IN MINIATURE

Though Pat Collins's Big Dipper was dismantled in the winter of 1950-1 and sent to Battersea Park, a miniature model was developed and displayed in Sutton. Over the years John Tidmarsh made four roller coasters. "I made a working model of the Big Dipper in balsa wood strips – about three feet long – which won me first prize in the K.E.G.S. hobbies exhibition in 1952. This model was followed in 1954 by a further giant working scenic railway model to my own design which was known as the 'Coronation Scot'. All the wood and other materials were purchased from Gill's

Another Pat Collin's amusement was the Jack and Jill Glide, which had a hill in the middle. (Rod Spooner)

toyshop on the corner of Holland Street and Birmingham Road in the centre of Sutton." Gill's management were so impressed with the model which showed what could be achieved from the products that they sold that "they exhibited it in their shop window for a month afterwards."

The idea of writing the history of the Sutton Miniature Railway came to John "in the early 1950s. So many times old 'gaffers' would hang over the fence for a chat while I was sitting in the loco cab waiting for passengers to arrive. They would open a conversation with "I remember this train when … and I regretted not writing down what they said." John continued "So I determined that one day I would write the line's history – it took over 30 years and a lot of research. I met some very interesting people in the process and I was very pleased with the result." ('The Sutton Coldfield 15" Gauge Railway', Plateway Press, 1990.)

S.M.R. SHOULD BE REBUILT

Dr. R. Harper, looking back at the 1950s, "considered the S.M.R. to be brilliant." With hindsight, he was aware that at the close of the 1962 season, the stock, traction and some buildings went into store somewhere in the Black Country. With much feeling and affection for the railway, he wrote that the Sutton Miniature Railway "should be rebuilt." Dreams sometimes come true. In addition to the railway, Roger wrote about the fun fair – in particular the switchback the helter-skelter and the memorable big dipper. Dr. Harper recalled "After the war I saw old ex-U.S. Army 'Ducks', landing craft on big wheels which were capable of going on water." He saw them used for pleasure rides on one of "the big lakes at the Crystal Palace, near the Clifton Road entrance."

BARRAGE BALLOON BEDROOM

Ken Jackson was at R.A.F. 216 M.U. at Sutton in 1951-52 and he remembered the S.M.R.. His R.A.F. duties were with the 'station party' based at Sutton Coldfield goods station. The R.A.F. caravan operated as an office just inside the gate and he did clerical and manual work "unloading and loading traffic for 216 M.U. with its associated documentation. The traffic mainly came in containers with cases of engines and tyres by the thousand." They used R.A.F. vehicles such as Scammels, ten-tonners and flatbeds. Ken said "We used the railway static crane for unloading railway containers."

R.A.F. 216 M.U. Station party in front of the goods yard wall, at Sutton. Second on the back row, Suttonian Phillip Peters, 3rd right is Ken Jackson. The last on the right was the railway checker. (Ken Jackson)

The railway foreman in charge of the goods yard was Tom Perks assisted by a checker. Miss Kitchen was the clerk in charge of the railway goods office. In the spring of 1951 "about 50 of us were billeted initially in an immense hanger used during World War Two to inflate and store barrage balloons." After six weeks they "were moved into wooden huts each sleeping about 20 men. The W.R.A.F.'s were in similar huts."

AVID ARCHER FANS

Ken continued, "Leisure activities included visits to the Empress and Odeon cinemas. There were, of course, plenty of pubs. On Wednesday afternoons they were free for recreation."

Amongst other things "we could go swimming at Kingstanding Baths or flying from Castle Bromwich. We were transported in R.A.F. covered trucks." The N.A.A.F.I. was a place "where we could meet, eat and drink." In the wooden huts "a tannoy system was used to broadcast radio in the evenings." What was a surprise to me was that Ken and his mates "were all avid Archer fans." The radio series was in its infancy in 1952 and I did not expect R.A.F. Service staff to follow such a programme.

A few years before when the wireless was the information and home entertainment medium, the kids would play in Jerome Road until about twenty to seven in the evening, then disappear to be rooted to the radio and follow every word of Dick Barton, special agent. After Ken's demob. in 1952, he resumed work on the railway as a class five clerk at Lawley Street Goods Station in Birmingham.

SUTTON PARK IS NOT PRIVATE

The type of crime reported in newspapers, particularly local ones, gives an indication of how serious certain offences were considered at the time. Some observers, aware of serving constables and their places of work in that period, may balance up the results knowing of zealous summon issuing police men and women. A Royal Road motorist was fined ten shillings for leaving the engine running whilst the car was unattended outside his house. The motorist blamed his wife! "He had called at his house for something and his wife had asked for assistance and he was detained for a few minutes."

Mr. H. W. Lyde, Chairman of Sutton Coldfield Magistrates Court wanted residents and visitors alike to be aware "that Sutton Park is not private". A number of learners practised in Sutton Park without a provisional licence or insurance. "There needed," he stressed, "to have a notice that Sutton Park is public."

A married woman was the cause of another offence. The court was told that she "had missed the last bus." Her husband, not wanting his other half stranded for the night, gave her a lift on his cycle back to the Sutton Park camp. They were each fined ten shillings for there "being two on a cycle."

One incident that some householders may have considered qualified for summons did not materialise – Holifast Road residents were enjoying a Sunday afternoon tea when they heard a loud crash. Looking around "they saw a large tail of a model aeroplane protruding from a bedroom window" of neighbours that were away on holiday. Both wings were ripped off in the crash. The petrol driven seven and half foot wing span plane was launched by a husband and his wife who told the media "It was a very windy day. The plane went higher and higher on the air current." They anticipated "we had said goodbye to it as it disappeared over New Oscott College." It crashed nearly two miles away. The owner's name was on the fuselage and the man later collected it!

THE A.A. MAN COMETH

Geoff Dixon joined the A.A. as a patrolman in 1952. He had always been "interested in mechanical things and had my own motorcycle from the age of 16." For a time he was employed "at an agricultural engineers." New A.A. employees "always had to attend the initial training course and periodically for refresher courses" at the Nottinghamshire A.A. Training School at Widmerpool Hall. Most of his patrol work was in the Birmingham area, working along the A446 between Moxhull and Kenilworth and, also, the Brownhills to Warwick section of the A452. Mr. Dixon recalled, "The A.A. in the period after the War consisted of a large number of ex-military personnel. In fact, the A.A. had its own corps of Redcaps within the Military Police." The A.A. discipline was strict with turnout having to be immaculate. He added, "Boots and leggings had to be polished with motorcycle equipment being kept spotless." The patrolmen kept to one motorcycle which they garaged "at home and were responsible for maintaining it." The machines were "upgraded from time to time and eventually had two way radios fitted."

MORE AGREEABLE MOTORISTS

The A.A. Patrol staff were saluting members and the badge displayed on any vehicle in the 1950s. Traffic was so much less, travelling "much slower and the motorist was a much more agreeable person than today's version" in Mr. Dixon's opinion. Honesty and trust were essential for the use of A.A. telephone boxes "as these were open private lines and could have been seriously abused by members." Now retired, Geoff looked back and said, "Members were always pleased to receive acknowledgement, asking for directions and information." Usually when a motorist "was assisted, there was a small gratuity passed to you and letters of appreciation were often sent to the office."

NATIONAL MEDIA ATTENTION

In an "unprecedented case", which caught the attention of local, regional and national curiosity, a P.C. informed the Sutton Court that a car driver was seen keeping his vehicle within the speed limit and not zigzagging, but using only one hand on the steering wheel leaving his free hand to "play his mouth organ!" In mitigation, the defendant told the magistrates "he travelled long distances for my firm, often playing while driving." The Bench dismissed the case, but the mouth organ player was still fined ten shillings for having no current licence and a further one pound for failing to produce a certificate of insurance.

DOCTOR OF CONSIDERABLE ABILITY

A local G.P. was fined £100 with an alternative of six months prison for obtaining "sums of money from patients which should have been free under the N.H.S." The General Medical Council, some while later, suspended judgement for twelve months.

In spite of the offence, the number of patients on the doctor's list increased! The defending counsel said that the doctor had achieved considerable success and could be described "as a doctor of some considerable ability." When the G.M.C judgement was announced, "The G.P., with head bowed, broke down."

MIDLAND CHAMPION BUS SPOTTER

A Bishop Vesey Grammar School pupil earned the title of 'Champion Bus Spotter of the Midlands.' There was an impression that his fastidious collecting of the complete Midland 'Red' fleet of 1,804 vehicles in 24 months would be difficult to equal by any other zealous bus spotter in the U.K.. Mr. D. M. Sinclair, the General Manager of the 'Red' presented sixteen-year-old Malcolm Cooper with a gift token for "his extraordinary feat in bus spotting." As far as the G.M. knew, "Malcolm was the only one of 10,000 M.'R'. badge holders to achieve such a record." Mr. Sinclair complimented the Sutton teenager on his "tenacity and skill", having seen the carefully kept books recording fleet changes, vehicle rebuilding or taken off road details.

Some of the buses Malcolm knew well from the Sutton garage were caught up in the traffic-congested diversions caused by the Sutton Parade reconstruction that had been going on for two months. It was announced the completion of the new island in front of the Parade gardens would give easier access from Sutton parade. The completed work included the camber of the stretch of road between the then Public Library and the Empress being removed, replaced by a new foundation. Main paths along the Parade were also being improved and the whole project completion was only "a month away."

PRANK TO PANIC

A thinly disguised act of vandalism, called a boyish prank, almost led to an animal's death. Ernest Fisher put his nine-year-old bay gelding out to graze in Sutton Park and some boys were believed to have chased the animal on to mud flats near Powell's Pool with the intention of causing the horse some distress. The Fire Service found the horse "was lying on its side and had sunk up to the ridge on its back." After three hours of careful planning which took into consideration the fearful, tiring horse, a sling was successfully slid beneath the animal and the horse raised to safe ground.

During the act of mercy, a fireman sustained a kick on the thigh and further injuries in the rescue that ended at 1.30a.m. on a Saturday morning.

Another animal owner was exercising his dog in Sutton Park and this led to a visit to Sutton Police Station. The duty police officer confirmed Mr. William Ward's find as a one-pound bomb – probably from the last war. The Stonehouse Road resident was relieved that there was no explosion.

WORLD WAR II RESIDUE

When I joined British Railways in 1950 it was a shock to receive a monthly package of food – it had been a reserved occupation in W.W.II. It was a further surprise that I had to pay for the sugar, fat, etc., but my mother was pleased to accept the provisions.

I think that it was in 1952 that another W.W.II phenomenon arrived at Four Oaks Railway Station without warning to some of the railway staff[1], which included me. Reference had been made to women being trained to take over signal box duties in the war at Sutton Park and elsewhere. This take over of pre-war male duties involved 20 females of various ages, abilities and sizes, yet seven years after the war they were still going strong and a match for any male gang.

The Walsall women's painting gang descended on a station like a flock of locusts with scaffolding, decorating equipment and an ample supply of paint and brushes.

Similarly to men, the routine preparatory work was done, followed by the agreed under coats and final coats of paint. All the stations and the depots that the W.W.P.G. completed showed a real improvement. During the occupation of Four Oaks station shouting, giggling, inter-group squabbling and military style swearing were all commonplace. The station staff believed that by interfering less, the quicker the W.W.P.G. would move on to their next group of unsuspecting railway colleagues at another venue, so the Four Oaks railway people tolerated the occupation. However, on one afternoon shift, when it came to my precious 3-4p.m.

---

1. Pages 16-17, Sutton Coldfield in the Forties.

lunchtime, some of the women pestered me in the foreman's hut as I tried to cook my baked beans. After a number of requests to leave me in peace, I left my snap, regrettably in a huff, and returned to work in the station buildings. After a while, the lady foreman came to say sorry on behalf of the gang and volunteered to cook my beans. I remained independent!

EIFFEL TOWER

The A.B.C. Minors' Club at the Empress came up with an idea that kept many Sutton and District children occupied in the evenings and weekends. Although parents had to deal with the children's and teenagers' frustration when the project was not going well, the eventual winner of the 1952 match-stick modelling competition was Malcolm Haynes with his model of the Eiffel Tower. Having used approximately 1,750 matchsticks, he then deliberately painted them with silver paint. His prize was free admission to the Saturday morning film shows for two months.

Eiffel Tower. Malcolm Haynes with his 1,750 matchsticks model that won a A. B. C. Minors Club competition at the Empress. (Bernard R. Haynes)

CHURCH GROVE FARM

John Abbott lived at Church Grove Farm in Rectory Road. Church Grove, with the Falcon Lodge farm, was sold by Mr. Frank Cattell to provide the land for the Falcon Lodge Estate and Mr. Abbott believed that Church Grove Farm was demolished in the early 1950s. The farm was on a hill above the Orchard House that belonged to the Hazel family – well known in the town as independent funeral directors.

John's grandfather was Charles Abbott, Mr. Cattell's bailiff for the whole estate, who lived and worked from Church Grove, which was a mixed farm. John recalled it had a milking herd of cows, pigs, chickens and two horses, Bob and Gypsy.

Incidentally, it was these horses that I was in charge of referred to on pages 109-111 in 'Sutton Coldfield in the Forties'. The arable side of the farm included wheat, potatoes and Swedes.

DAD'S COLLEAGUE

Mr. Dick Shears, the cowman at Church Grove, was the colleague of my cowman father, Albert Bassett, at the Falcon Lodge Farm. After their dairy work, they at times worked together on estate activities that needed more manpower. Both Dick and Dad collected the milk by hand from their respective herds, "Then cooled and stored it in churns for collection by Mr. O. Eaton who then distributed the milk locally." All the conveyance of products and equipment around the farm was by the two carthorses.

John said the only mechanical power on the estate was a very old Fordson tractor which powered the threshing machine at harvest time. "All hands were required for this hot and thirsty work. The main refreshment for this work was cold tea with no milk," John remembered. My brother David and I benefited in the late forties from the long hours worked by Dad, Dick and John's granddad. Sometime after 9p.m., Dad arrived home after a 15-hour day, exhausted, thirsty and hungry. David and I gladly assisted him devouring his well-earned dinner, which was accompanied with an ample supply of Falcon Lodge farm-fresh vegetables. Whichever way Dad went to or returned from work on his cycle from Jerome Road to the farm, he met an incline.

Probably the most severe was Reddicap Hill which Dad used to climb about 5.30a.m. most mornings.

NOISY CELEBRITY

A favourite drag queen, noted for explosive shrieks and fast banter, presented birthday cards and sweets to A.B.C. Minors at the Empress. Arthur Lucan, under the guise of Old Mother Riley, entertained the youngsters with a short sketch. 'She' was appearing at the Dudley Hippodrome and a Worrall picture showed Old Mother Riley, his understudy, Roy Roland, with Gale Douglas, who played Mrs. Ginnochie, alongside A.B.C. Minors and the Empress manager, Tim Whittaker.

SPOTLIGHT ON UPPER HOLLAND ROAD

The Midland 'Red' monthly staff journal had a two page centre spread on the Sutton Garage, the only one at that time with a post-war extension. Long serving staff were: Mr. N. L. Cole, Engineering Superintendent, with more than thirty years; the traffic superintendent, Mr. F. A. Kerrison, with nearly 25 years; and driver G. A. Horton who joined the company in 1920. Other folk mentioned were: J. and F. G. Smith; H. Norris; W. T. Garner; A. E. Lakin and F. Robinson.

EDITORIAL COMMENT – NATIONAL T.V. ADVERTISING

The News editorial comment was often on a national issue affecting local life. In June the Editor approved of a White Paper policy allowing for sponsored T.V. in competition with the Corporation's programmes. This provided an early opportunity, which might otherwise have been lost, of establishing a wise and stable system of safeguards against abuse of the service. The Editor thought that competition would not lead to a "free-for-all scramble for audiences in which taste and decency will be sacrificed."

Between October 1951 and March 1952 there had been a half a million increase in T.V. licences. Locally though, during that period, 45 viewers were prosecuted "for working sets without licences." Although there had been many pre-war radio broadcasts from Sutton, a temporary T.V. studio was set up in Sutton Town Hall, described as one of "the most elegant buildings in the Royal Town." Residents were invited to put questions to a sports panel with the proceedings televised. Two names taking part were known to many sports fans – Marjorie Pollard, the international hockey player, and Peter Cranmer, the sprinter and sporting journalist.

TOO MANY COOKS

Rod Spooner arrived at 216 M.U. as an L.A.C. cook and during his two and half year stay became a corporal cook. Rod was in-charge of a shift in the Airmen's Mess. "The set-up in the mess was unusual," and hilarious for observers at times. The Warrant Officer in charge was a W.R.A.F., a swearing, drinking and fun loving Mancunian, whereas the sergeant, also a W.R.A.F., was a strict Welsh Chapel type who tried to get the men to Bible classes. Rod wrote, "They were two contrasts and used to clash!"

All the cooks were men with some W.R.A.F. orderlies. In his leisure time, Rod went Barn and Country Dancing at Maney Hall, dancing at the Abbey, Erdington, and Modern Dancing at the Palace, Erdington, the Locarno and West End in the Birmingham City centre. He remembered, "Catching a tram from Birmingham late Saturday nights and having to walk from the Chester Road Tram Terminus to Whitehouse Common."

COOLEST PLACES

Shortly after the News recorded a torrential downpour in the Town, causing three to four foot flooding in South Parade and Jockey Road districts, Sutton was in the middle of a heat wave. Freres recommended the place to avoid the heat was to walk in the 'country' areas of Sutton Park or relax in the air-conditioned Odeon cinema. A celebrity of radio connected with country life and walking around his farm opened a féte in Four Oaks. Harry Oakes, the actor who played Dan Archer, spoke of the character details that each of the Archers' cast were given. As Dan, he represented a 54 year old who had been brought up perfectly, "From a church infant he became a choir-boy." Harry played a farmer, "Listed as a staunch Conservative!"

QUEEN STREET RECUPERATION

In the 1940s Arthur and Bernard Chamberlain were sorry to lose Harold Groves from their developing greengrocery business on the corner of Queen Street and the Parade.

In 1952 Harold and Doreen left their joint Officer posts at the Bradford Salvation Army Citadel when Harold had a long illness. They returned with young Wesley to the Queen Street home of Doreen's parents. Harold received treatment in "Good Hope which was just a large house in those days situated approximately where the present hospital's A&E is located." Some time later, after recuperating at home, Harold returned with brother Frank to Chamberlains and Harold soon became fruit and vegetables departmental manager.

Wesley recalled that he lived with his mum and dad at "my grandparent's house in Queen Street. As a six year old boy I used to help the milkman leading his horse from Newhall Street round Lower Queen Street and back into Queen Street." He was also allowed to help at "Chamberlains particularly on Saturdays when I would push a hand truck loaded with empty crates." Without "transport it was very difficult to get to the nearest S.A. in Erdington or Aston, so the family worshipped at Duke Street Hall where my mother attended as a girl." Thinking about N.H.S. provision,

Chamberlains, Mr Harold Groves became the fruit and vegetables department manager at Chamberlains parade shop. (Birmingham Library Services)

Wesley's first recollection of a doctor "was D. F. Amos whose surgery was opposite the Royal Hotel in the High Street. I attended Anstey College in Chester Road, Boldmere, in the early 1950s for exercise treatment to ease my asthma." The exercises included lying on a mat on the wooden floor and "having to pick up a bean bag from behind my head using only my toes. I also remember attending the clinic in Holland Street to take polio vaccination on a sugar cube."

GOOD HOPE MAKES A DIFFERENCE

Dennis Wilkinson remembered the old house, known as Good Hope, which was pulled down and replaced with the development of what is now known as Good Hope Hospital. At that time, "The wards were single storey buildings and most of them are still in existence. Further developments resulted in the building of a central block with an upper floor which became wards 14, 15, 16 and 17. Amongst the early surgeons were Mr. Beatson and Mr. Cozens-Hardy. One of the physicians, Dr. Dennis Gibbs, had a great interest in the development of the Gastro camera.

Mr. Wilkinson assisted Dr. Gibbs with illustrations for a small leaflet on the subject." At about the same time, there appeared from Japan a "beautiful, very professional book on the same subject." Dr. Bass, later to become Professor Bass, also introduced the Hyperbaric Oxygen unit for treatment of certain types of ulcer. "The equipment consisted of a Perspex 'coffin' and the patient lay in this for the duration of the treatment. Oxygen was pumped into the Unit with a positive pressure and resulted in a high oxygen intake by the patient." Dennis told me, "I saw many ulcers remarkably healed by this form of treatment."

ON-CALL RADIOGRAPHER

In later years, with the opening of the Good Hope Accident and Emergency Department and the employment of resident medical staff, the hospital began taking emergency work for the whole of the Lichfield, Hammerwich, Tamworth and Sutton Coldfield areas. Initially, the on-call radiographer remained at home for the period of the duty and later at the hospital in an 'On-call room'. Because of demand and geographical problems, the Victoria Hospital, Lichfield, and the General Hospital, Tamworth, also had an on-call service, but the radiographers stayed at home and were not called in as frequently as at the Good Hope.

LADY OWEN PRESENTATION

The outline history of the Boldmere Brotherhood recorded that the old two-person manual reed organ, which had continued use in the Boldmere Methodist Church for many years, was getting into a bad state of repair. Eventually, a second hand pipe instrument, including electric blower, pedal board and bench, was bought for one hundred and forty five pounds.

In 1952 the Walmley Boys Brigade had grown to 61 members. Eddie Maddox rejoined the company - taking over the leadership from David Holt. A proud moment for the company was when Sergeant Michael Russell received the first King's Badge from Lady Owen.

LOCAL VALUATION APPEALS

Sutton was privileged to host the first demonstration of its kind, anywhere in the U.K. at any Cine Society, of the latest 16m.m. three-dimensional colour films. It was expected that the unprecedented interest would be a milestone in the history of amateur cinematography.

Another significant event in the Borough's 1952 history was the largest number of people concerned in a single appeal to appear before a local sitting of the Local Valuation Court in Sutton Council House (since the passing of the Local Government Act in 1948). For the residents living in Pilkington Avenue, St.Bernard's Road and Monkseaton Road, four appeals were dismissed and 12 residents granted reductions. The grounds for appealing for a valuation reduction included concrete structures, T.A. base drilling, pylons, and in some instances "concern about the orphanage and its activities."

REOPEN WARTIME BRICKYARDS

A shortage of bricks was slowing down house building in the Borough and Mr. T. Porter, the Borough Surveyor, informed the News, "There is a very bad shortage of bricks at the moment." The consequences of the shortage were "all our contractors are being held up." Builders in the area put the shortage down to three reasons" the small number of brick manufacturers in the country; "brickyards closing in the August Bank holiday and the employees' annual holidays;" and the greater demand on bricks during the summer months when building was not as badly affected by the weather.

Butlers, one of the main contractors on the Falcon Lodge estate, "Believed the answer was to reopen many of the brickyards which were closed down during the war due to the contraction of the industry." Sutton's Housing Committee wanted the Falcon Lodge Estate to be completed in three years. The Borough also had a demand for one bed roomed flats as there were a number of single businesswomen living alone in the area.

MINISTRY OF WORKS DILEMMA

The Ministry of Works was "receiving a large number of applications from members of the public in all parts of the country, presumably including Suttonians, for seats in the Governments stands on the 1953 Coronation route." David Eccles, the Minister of Works, coming to the defence of a hard-pressed staff announced, "Seats on Government stands for the United Kingdom will be allocated through national bodies and organisations covering, as far as possible, every aspect of national life. It was up to the bodies themselves how many seats are allocated."

PREMATURE DEATHS
News writer Freres was taken up with the premature deaths of tortoises locally. A local naturalist noted that tortoises were being imported from a hot climate under very poor conditions just as they were emerging from hibernation. The specialist informed Freres "The tortoises cannot eat after hibernation until they have had a good drink."

HEALTH BUILDING – ENVIRONMENT DESTROYED
Due to Dr. Preston's very progressive policies in child welfare, there was evidence that cod liver oil and orange juice was "making the race taller." However, local mothers were encouraged to "claim their child's entitlement." The Borough's M.O.H. enthusiastic pursuit of child health practices led to "several clinics being opened throughout the Borough."

It was also in October that the Government announced the end of tea rationing and Britain's first Atomic bomb had "been successfully exploded" in the Monte Bello Islands, off the north west coast of Australia.

RE–EVALUATION OF THE THREE Rs
The Riland-Bedford School was the venue for a re-evaluation of the 3 Rs in the curriculum of primary and secondary schools for the education section of the Warwickshire County Teachers' Association. A similar course of lectures had been held at Leamington. The main conclusions were: (i) The need to reaffirm the fundamental importance of the three Rs in any system of education; (ii) The need for a dynamic role of the teacher in teaching; and (iii) they hoped teachers would give full consideration to the proper emphasis

Potential Sutton Manhood. Riland-Bedford Teacher, Mr. Wright with thirtyfour adolescent students. (John Abbott)

on their own position and value in and out of the classroom without which no teaching can be effective. An N.U.T. official said "There is no antagonism between some of our modern trends and the older arts and crafts we attempted to teach."

SUTTON COLDFIELD TELEVISION MAST

Patrons of the new cinema in Paradise Street, Birmingham, saw a 16m.m. film on the local television mast. To gain access to the top of the mast a lift took five minutes to reach six hundred feet. To reach the inspection point, required a one hundred and ten foot climb by ladder from the lift. Sutton Coldfield's record of being the tallest T.V. mast in the world was now shared with Kirk-O'Shotts, Holme Moss and Wenvoe.

The Good Hope Annex referred to by Dennis Wilkinson in 1952 is mentioned in a November issue of the Sutton Coldfield News. The account speaks of the building being erected, providing "extended facilities to the Sutton Coldfield Hospital" on the Birmingham Road. The Good Hope site was "capable of dealing with serious casualties in road accidents." It would ensure more prompt treatment of injuries than the present practice of road accident casualties being taken to the Birmingham Accident Hospital.

THEORY INTO PRACTICE

Blanche Allen enjoyed Sutton and its people and "made many friends as well as my husband's many friends." She found shopping in Sutton took a long time. "It was difficult going shopping along the Parade with Tom," she advised me. "We were stopped every few yards by people who knew him and those who wanted horticultural advice," she added.

Mrs. Allen found "My own pregnancy went well and I was well looked after by Dr. Violet Parks of Birmingham Road, Wylde Green." Paul was born at Oakhurst where she had introduced to mothers' relaxation techniques during physiotherapy sessions, which were frowned upon by senior management there. Blanche was in labour when Matron and her deputy were at lunch "when things began to happen. They dashed upstairs to see how I performed, using my birthing techniques, but I did very well and cocked a snook at them!"

DREADED DENTAL VISITS

Many Suttonians would probably have been able to identify with David Gumbley's dread of visiting his dentist. The practitioner "never seemed to appreciate youngsters and the atmosphere was always one of brusque tolerance." A popular place to forget the dentist and meet with other schoolmates "was Patterson's café where you went through the shop and down a short flight of stairs."

Apparently a treat was a visit to Trow's Milk Bar for an ice cream after shopping at Roses. David associated the Seven Hour Cleaners on the Parade with "a chemical smell of cleaning agent and a big rotary cleaner."

INFORMAL STREETLY STATION

In the early 1950s David often went train spotting on a Saturday morning to New Street Station. He cycled to Streetly Station for the 8.16a.m. and left his bike on the platform. "To buy a ticket you always walked straight into the booking office where there was a roaring fire – nobody used the booking window!" The train was always "two compartment coaches hauled by a 2-6-2 tank locomotive such as 40085 or 40173," both locos from Walsall shed.

David's friend from Jerome Road, Lionel Goodenough, joined at Sutton Park and they used to wave to Lionel's mother as the train sped down the bank towards Penns. They returned on the 12.20p.m. from Platform 8 and the train was always "corridor stock which we considered the height of comfort."

Their favourite train spotting location in Sutton was at Old Bank Place, just off the High Street opposite Railway Road. From the wall they could observe trains on the Midland and L.N.W.R. lines. However, the "local residents did not approve and we did not return after a few evenings." The Five O'clock goods on the Sutton Park Line was a train worth waiting for because "it could be hauled by a locomotive running in after an overhaul at Crewe."

THE BRUMMIES

Gerry Taylor revealed how some teenagers in the 1950s were willing to walk to places of leisure rather than catch a bus or a train. He wrote, "We used to walk to Perry Barr Speedway on a Saturday night when it was safe to do this sort of thing. My, how things have changed!" The 'Brummies' team "consisted of Alan 'Whacker' Hunt, Doug Davies from South Africa, Ivor Davis from Tamworth, Eric Boothroyd, and Tiger Hart from Perry Barr." To Gerry they were "fabulous days - we'd collect empty pop bottles and take them back for the 3d!!!" A few of us from Duke Street Hall were 'Brummie' supporters, but not being energetic types, caught the 107 bus from outside the Dog which passed the speedway track. We proudly wore the yellow and red scarves and enthusiastically used rattles on the open terraces – coughing from the shale and fumes as the four riders fought for the first place on the fairly tight circuit. One teenage girl confided in me years later that she thought it was "exceptionally noisy, but she looked forward to the 'eats'."

On an away 'Brummies' excursion one Bank Holiday, on returning from Belle Vue, Manchester, there was no lighting in one section of the train. With my two years' knowledge of carriage light equipment, I tried to put the lights on, but regrettably I managed to turn all the lights off in the ten or so carriages! Hastily I remembered how to switch them all back on and moved swiftly out of the empty guard's compartment. In addition to the 'Brummie' race programmes, it became critical to read at least one of the weekly speedway magazines to find out how Aussie Graham Warren of the 'Brummies' was getting on down-under during our close season.

DUKE STREET HALL YOUTH OUTREACH

Although I was a soft target for teenage bullies, regrettably, in order to be noticed I became in my teens a big mouthed nuisance at the Duke Street Hall Covenanter Boys' Club for thirteen to eighteen year olds. My behaviour in retrospect was probably on the same level as Reverend Wilbert Awdry's 'troublesome trucks'. The leaders, not unlike the fat controller, gave me a severe reprimand and a warning that any further disruptive behaviour would lead to a suspension. Instead of toeing the line, I was worse and got suspended. Having missed the companionship and fellowship of other lads and the leadership, I modified my attitudes and behaviour sufficiently to be later re-admitted.

As a national Christian Boys' Organisation we met other Covenanter groups in the West Midlands for football, table tennis and rallies. The Christian teaching was

1952, Duke Street Covenanters 5-a-side team, at Witton Lakes. (Author)

challenging and the leaders were good witnesses to their faith. Although coming from a working class background, the majority of the Duke Street Hall members were middle class, accepting me and showing care and friendship for me and my family. I remember that every Easter, Norman Whitehouse and family who attended Duke Street Hall went on holiday. For my family, when money was available, it would be in the proper holiday time of August. What it probably showed, but I had no insight at the time, was that Mr. Whitehouse and family had stressful, responsible work to cope with that was foreign to me. Many years later I recognised that, probably without knowing, the Duke Street Hall members related to me in a middle class way – accepting in a middle class way my working class position and lowly status of a railway porter. Their ways of thinking, questioning and decision making were later to be a positive contribution in pursuing my further and higher education opportunities.

SUNDAY SCHOOL BUS SERVICE

The News columnist Freres was advised by the correspondent from Duke Street Hall, Mr. Frank Wilday, that Duke Street Mission was a very live church. Until a suitable temporary building could be erected, for a three-month period, an open air Sunday school was held on the Falcon Lodge between July and September, 1952 and about 50 children were given free bus transport from the Falcon Lodge Estate to Duke Street Hall each Sunday afternoon at other times. Mr. Wilday pointed out that the Sutton congregation had taken a very keen interest in making some provision in meeting the spiritual needs of the young folk on the estate.

NO LATER SHOPPING

The introduction of regular late closing of Sutton Coldfield shops could happen, warned some members of the Town's Chamber of Commerce, if such facilities began for Christmas 1952. Mr.Howes, the Hon. Secretary, reported the matter had been thoroughly discussed. It was felt that "too many difficulties were involved. What extra business that might be brought in would not compensate for the extra work involved." The existing closing

Late night shopping. Not too far from Betty Pitchford's late night Christmas opening hours for men, stood the 1948 closed Provident Dispensary on the Junction of Rectory Road, Coleshill Street and Trinity Hill. (Birmingham Library Services)

hours would remain – recommending late opening to 7p.m. on Fridays. The proposal for the late Christmas shopping opening times, some considered, "was the thin edge of the wedge."

However, Betty Pitchford, at 53 Rectory Road, encouraged men to a late night shopping event at her shop on 23rd December, 5-8p.m., by saying "Purchase Christmas gifts for your lady".

6d A BUNCH OF HOLLY

The council took some stick from working class folk in 1952 by recommending charging 6d. for a bunch of Sutton Park holly. After much debate the proposal was defeated and the tradition of not charging continued. Some councillors thought it was reasonable "for people to pay a small amount to cover costs." To buy a similar bunch, to the 8,000 bunches of holly distributed from the Park, cost 2s.6d or 3s. in the shops.

The cost of labour, alone, to the taxpayer was about £200. Years before, I had traipsed back from Blackroot Pool depot a number of times along with other children from Jerome Road. We dragged our prickly bunch of holly behind us to the main gate, down Park Road, across the Parade, along Victoria Road, down Upper Holland Road, Kathleen Road and victoriously to Jerome Road and our delighted mothers. I am not sure how many berries survived the bumpy journey!

BUS STOPS ON THE MOVE

In "deference to the wishes of property owners" and other people near the traffic island at the top of Mill Street, Walsall Corporation agreed to a new terminus in Victoria Road. It hoped to site a stop for outgoing buses near the junction of Coleshill Street and High Street. A News letter writer congratulated the No.6 Walsall service provider for the additional lunchtime services. Another writer pointed out that "many buses are already using Victoria Road. Could the Walsall outward buses use South parade similar to the West Bromwich Corporation terminus No 25?" In the realms of public transport, former Sutton Coldfield (L.N.W.R.) stationmaster, Frederick W. Rogers, died at 62. Mr. Rogers retired through ill health and lived on the Falcon Lodge. At one time he was captain of the Tudor Bowling Club.

Sutton's oldest resident at that time, Mrs. Diana Dain, died aged 103 years old. She resided in Sutton from 1892 and was the widow of High Street draper, Mr. Major, who had died in 1929. Mrs. Dain left three sons and a daughter.

REASONABLE SHOP PRICES

According to the local News reporters, pre-Christmas Church services and Nativity plays "were exceedingly well attended." Sutton Coldfield shopkeepers thought the

1952 Christmas was the "brightest since pre-war days with shortages only in a few commodities." There was a wider and more varied selection of goods to suit every pocket. "Prices are definitely more reasonable," is how one shopkeeper summed up the general opinion of most local traders.

A letter from a health adviser recommended readers grow their own fruit and vegetables, with vegetable compost well dug in. Using such methods prevented the poisoning of our food like "the chemicalised food."

John Platt identified four top of the pop songs in 1952 as 'Auf Wiedersehn Sweetheart', 'Here in my Heart', 'You belong to me' and 'Wheel of Fortune'.

CORONATION CELEBRATIONS – NOT BEER AND BUNS

Some ecclesiastical personages and civic officials had criticised people "for taking advantage of the planned 1953 Coronation as a beer and bun do and waste public money."

One commentator thought such critics "lacked imagination." People, it was suggested by the pro-Coronation interviewee, had arranged activities for their children and had focussed on the "pleasures of entertaining" the younger members of the Sutton Coldfield communities.

Chapter Three

1953 – CORONATION AND CONSCRIPTION

"APARTHEID – A NECESSARY EVIL"

This contentious viewpoint was held, according to the Sutton Coldfield News, by a Suttonian after nearly a year's residence in South Africa. The local man had travelled extensively in the Union where the population at the time was ten million non-whites and two and half million whites. The former Sutton Coldfield parishioner considered "To sum up, if it were not for the unsettling misconstrued reports about South Africa which are starting to make certain people wonder what sort of country it is, I would say that it is one of the best places in the world in which to live."

SUTTONIAN VICTIM OF TRAM CRASH

A two-tram collision at Aston resulted in three injured passengers one of whom, an eighteen-year-old from Welwyndale Road, had facial cuts. Witnesses told of a "terrific bump as one tram ran into the back of the other." The ends of the trams folded in and glass and woodwork were showered over the road. At one time more than 20 trams on the Erdington, Short Heath and Tyburn routes were held up before the damaged trams were shunted into sidings at Fort Dunlop. A nearby café supplied tea for the shaken passengers.

SUTTON FAMILY ESCAPES DAKOTA CRASH

Within two weeks of the tram incident an Air Lingus Dakota airliner crashed near Alcester. Just before the crash an airhostess, who was so anxious about possible passenger injuries and fatalities, knelt down in the plane and asked everybody to pray.

A Sutton Coldfield Rugby Club player, a former Fleet Air Arm pilot, helped his son out through a large hole torn in the side of the plane whilst his wife managed to climb out of the fuselage with their nine-month-old son. The Coleshill Road family were returning from a fortnight's holiday in Dublin where they had spent Christmas with relatives.

BOMB THREAT TO SIR JOHN MELLOR, M.P. FOR SUTTON

Under suspicious circumstances, a bomb type used in W.W.II was found hanging inside a shed at the Hampshire home of Sir. John and Lady. Mellor. The live 'butterfly' bomb could explode "at the very slightest vibration" and was removed by an Army Bomb Disposal Squad whose captain safely exploded it.

POWER OF THE PRESS

The letter columns in all newspapers, including the Sutton Coldfield News, can sometimes reveal the hearty support of readers for a news story, but, at the other end of the scale, readers can show uncontrolled aggression. Reading through over 800 issues of the News in the years 1945-1960, the power and influence of the press was obvious. Presumably the reporter of a councillor's sweeping accusations relating to an educational subject was aware the story would cause grief and heart-searching, plus claims for solid evidence from the enraged councillor.

Such a story in 1953 also reminded readers of the power and authority of the councillors that the people had elected. Regular column writer, Freres, later considered "the allegations were unsubstantiated, but that it was likely that unnecessary hurt had been caused."

FARMERS' LAND CONCERN

Sutton and District farmers expressed their dismay that "scrub and waste land was being ignored whilst good fertile land was being used for building purposes." Such was the growing demand for good land "that the acreage of many farms in the District had been drastically cut and some of the best agricultural land had been lost."

According to Messrs. H. Donald Dixon, there had been a drop in the value of both older and modern types of housing. The lowering of prices was linked to an increasing shortage of money, high taxation and the consequent difficulty of saving. Building Societies and Insurance companies were prepared to lend "80% of the valuation figure on good freehold or leasehold properties." The Estate Agents noted a surprising drop in the values of farms during 1952, yet building land for residential and industrial purposes was becoming scarce.

HOME OF REST CLOSED

In January 1953 an important community resource closed due to "changing social conditions and the difficulties of present-day finance." The Home of Rest in Tudor Hill said "Good-Bye" to its last guests. The Matron of the last fifteen years, Miss Preston, received a cheque in recognition of her care and service. Mrs. C.A. Sheldon, who presented the cheque, was the only member of the committee who had served the full sixty years since the home started!

STALKING OF SECRETARY

A 51 year-old Boldmere secretary felt that she had been stalked by a thief because, having put her bag behind her desk at work, on returning from an adjacent room, she heard someone running away and her handbag, containing twenty pounds in wages, had been stolen.

Although the approximate age of the thief was not stated, major juvenile crime in the Borough's area had risen 100% in 1952 from five to ten cases with minor crimes moving up from five to eight (still not as bad as some other parts of Warwickshire).

From nil in 1951, there had been three motoring and four cycling offences in the following year, whereas motor-cycling offences went the other way from four in 1951 to nil in 1952. Compare with the 21st century!

ANTHRAX OUTBREAK

The police assisted at a Grange Lane farm after a case of Anthrax had been confirmed among the cattle and the farm was closed down. The farmer said "the cow was worth about seventy pounds." He did not think that there was any compensation for stock losses due to anthrax. Most of his stock "was supplied to the Ministry of Food."

There was also police involvement when a lady was found drowned in two and half feet of water in Blackroot Pool. Corporation boatmen recovered the body and the Coroner advised that the deceased had left a note "which quite clearly showed what she intended to do."

EAST COAST FLOODING

Although the east and west coast seaside resorts were some hours away from Sutton Coldfield both by rail or road, the Mayor of Sutton's appeal for the National Flood and Tempest Distress Fund had raised £3,450 by 19th February. Ten days or so earlier 283 people were known to have died in the east coast flooding, with 50 still missing.

A growing number of working class families in the Royal Town managed a camping, caravan or bed and breakfast holiday with Wales, Somerset, Lincolnshire and the Fylde coast proving regular favourites. From the Park Road garage, Hastilow's 'Tudor Rose' coaches provided weekly summer services to the North Wales towns of Rhyl, Colwyn Bay and Llandudno.

A FAMILY SEASIDE HOLIDAY

In the early nineteen fifties, I had my first family holiday with my brother, David, and my parents. Although a few families in Jerome Road had vehicles by the early

1950s, the majority used public transport and it was an exciting adventure for us to reach Rhyl using a Hastilow coach. We hired a modest caravan on one of Rhyl's many caravan sites – our site was situated on the Kinmel Bay side of a road bridge across a local river. Apparently, I instructed David, then only ten years old, on how to fish with a reel and a hook. He still blames me for not catching any fresh fish which would have been welcomed by my mother to supplement our self-catering budget!

Broad's Travel Bureau, situated at the Chester Road Tram Terminus, were agents for Hastilow's North Wales service. Using other coach companies as well, Broad's were able to offer weekly departures to the Lake District, Scotland and the Isle of Man plus day, half-day and evening excursions.

The author's brother David, enjoyed the family's first holiday in a caravan at Rhyl. (Bassett Family Collection)

ROYAL DEATH

Just over two months before the Coronation of Queen Elizabeth II, the Mayor and Town Clerk of Sutton sent a telegram to her referring to the death of Queen Mary. The local leaders spoke of "Queen Mary's grace, sympathy and understanding which endeared her to the hearts of the people." The News considered "Queen Mary's life is already more than a tradition that must, and will be, maintained." Anglican and Methodist clergy officiated at the United Memorial Service.

WAR EMERGENCY HOSPITALS

Even almost eight years after the end of the Second World War in Europe, the fragility of peace within the nation was exposed by the Civil Defence First Aid Service plans which designated the Sutton Coldfield Hospital and the Good Hope Annexe as 'Cushion hospitals' to deal with emergency cases in the event of war.

Such 'Cushion hospitals' were situated on the fringes of a 'Key area' such as Birmingham. In the plans the two local hospitals "would be equipped to deal with all types of cases, but only urgent ones would be sent." Once the patient's critical period had passed, he or she would be sent to an unnamed Base hospital.

Over the years the Civil Defence Corps had difficulty recruiting members, but there was a slight increase in Sutton membership, probably due to the excellent life-saving work of the C.D. Rescue squads during the east coast flood disaster and the Harrow and Wealdstone train crash.

HIGHEST BUS FARES IN ENGLAND

A local Councillor told residents a fact which many had suspected for years! The Councillor informed Boldmere West Ward Residents' Association the Midland 'Red' bus company had frankly admitted that "they charged what they liked, where they could." The high fares were considered appropriate because Sutton Coldfield was known nationally for its affluent majority of residents. The Councillor continued "there is no doubt that here we pay the highest fares in the country." However, the Councillor partly blamed the situation on the previous Council representatives. He told constituents that "unlike many other towns, due to the short-sightedness of his predecessors, the Council receives no money from the bus company for the use of the Town's roads." [1]

LITTLE ASTON HALL SOLD

After the sale of Little Aston Hall, the Midland Divisional Manager of the Esso Petroleum Company assured a Sutton News reporter "that nothing would be done which might cause a deterioration of neighbouring property values." It took Esso two years to complete the purchase with the Hall becoming the Midland Division Administrative Headquarters. Previously, departments had been "housed in four different city addresses, thus efficiency had been increased." The staff would benefit from better amenities, including welfare facilities and outdoor sports pitches.

VISITING CHILDREN IN HOSPITAL

A Streetly mother, Mrs. F. Yardley, was dissatisfied with the children's visiting policy operated by many Midlands hospitals. She had found "that in Birmingham hospitals, except in very grave cases, parents were not allowed to visit their children on a daily basis." Against considerable bureaucracy, Mrs. Yardley organised a petition requesting that a recent recommendation, by no less than the Minister of Health, "that daily visiting of children should be allowed, whenever possible, in all hospitals in the Midlands region." Many parents and families, identifying with her cause, gave the mother support. Mrs. Yardley told a News reporter that the public support for her petition "had been tremendous." It was to be sent to the Midland Regional Hospital Board. Apparently, hospitals in the Lichfield, Tamworth and Sutton Coldfield group already allowed visits "under control." Mrs. Yardley and her supporters were advised later that children could be visited daily in Birmingham hospitals, subject to safeguards against infection.

---

1. *The Midland 'Red' began operating Sutton services in 1913. See page 8 of 'Wheels around Sutton, Lichfield and Tamworth', Brewin Books, 1997.*

PARK FORESTER

James Parker, the Park Forester from 1930, retired at the end of March, 1953.

Presumably, he was concerned, like Alderman W.E. Lawley, "that Wyndley Pool was growing smaller because of the encroachment of weeds." The Alderman thought that "the Corporation should buy the tackle and do the work themselves, rather than waiting until the ducks could not swim on the pool."

A new Queen's Coppice, planted in the Park to commemorate the Coronation, included trees planted by representatives of 19 schools.

A Sutton Park staff member, known for his keen interest in wildlife in the Park, was Alfred Warren who had seen two specimens of Canada Geese staying six days during March at Bracebridge. "They became quite tame, taking scraps of bread from the shore." One of the rarest visitors, last noted in 1949, was a Hen Harrier seen over Powell's Pool in a brief visit in 1953. Other sightings in April included five Black Ducks, a common Scoter on Bracebridge, and two velvet Scoter duck on Longmoor Pool.

CORONATION TOURS

Hastilow's responded to local public interest in the Coronation by running special tours to London each day during Coronation week. During the remainder of June they operated thrice weekly tours to the capital. Coaches left Sutton at midnight, picking up at Erdington at 12.15a.m. with the fare being 20/3 return.

One wonders if the Coronation celebrations inspired the formation of the Sutton Coldfield British Legion band. Three hundred pounds worth of silver instruments had been bought, but until funds were raised for ornate uniforms, the members wore decorative khaki battledress.

DAY RETURNS

British Railways introduced new experimental Day Return tickets on the Lichfield –Sutton Coldfield-Birmingham New Street line. Specimen fares were Sutton to Lichfield City 1s/7d, Four Oaks 4d, Erdington 9d, and Birmingham New Street 1s/3d respectively. Two weeks after the introduction of the new fares "the Sutton trains were crowded with people flocking back to the railway." The Midland Committee of the Railway Development Association, which organised the new ticket structure, said "all we need now are more coaches and enlarged stocks of tickets!"

O.H.M.S.

One of the benefits of working on the railways, which helped to compensate for low wages, was a limited number of annual free rail tickets that could be used to travel to any part of the U.K. railway network. Also, an employee could have an unlimited number of 'privilege' (sometimes referred to as 'quarter fare') tickets. Both these types of tickets were to be of great value to me in the next couple of years.

The dreaded envelope, clearly marked O.H.M.S., arrived and gave instructions to have an X-ray in preparation for my National service. I joined a queue of 18-year-old-plus young men lining up for the appointment at the Radiography Department in Corporation Street, Birmingham. The first major step towards serving Queen and Country was passed.

NEW PARK FORESTER

Mr. Allen "was appointed to the post of Park forester on the first of April 1953, the year of our Queen's Coronation, lived in the Park Lodge, Park Road, a seven day a week job". Some of Tom's "projects included the Vesey Gardens which needed much work doing on them. We lowered the stone walls along the front of the gardens, resoiling most of the beds and each year we had fine displays of spring and summer bedding. Many letters of appreciation were seen in the local press." Mr. Allen continued, "The fence at the War Memorial was removed and a York stone wall erected." The gardens opposite the Dog Inn and traffic islands at Four Oaks station, Boldmere Road and Beggars Bush all benefited from new concepts in their appearance. Mr. Allen remembered "The Boddington Gardens were constructed and the borders were planted with herbaceous perennials and shrubs."

Sutton's new Park Forester, Mr. Tom Allen, with an exhibit at the Town's Flower Show. (Birmingham Post and Mail / Mr. T. Allen)

FORTY BRIDGES INTRODUCTION

The park forester was always pleased to see the "Great Crested Grebes on Bracebridge pool and the large flocks of Redstarts in the Hollyhurst area." Tom considered that Sutton Park at the time of his work in the park was perhaps the "best area in the country to see clouds of Holly Blue butterflies." Drosera rotundifolia was to be found around the stream which feeds Blackroot pool.

At Tom's instigation the Red Oak was introduced into pool Hollies by the forty bridges. He told me "The English Oak *Zuercus Robur* never did well in the sand gravelly soil and became stag headed and unsightly in time." The Red Oak variety "is much more tolerant of the soil conditions found in the park."

Mr. Allen alerted visitors to the park, that if they were near the older oak trees, and stood still and listened, "they may hear something champing away at the foliage." It would probably be the Tortrix Moth, Tortrix Viridana often called the Green Oak-roller perhaps the best known defoliator of trees. "Its caterpillars", Tom informed me, "cause the leaves to roll up, become shrivelled and fall." The trees produced more leaves, but their growth was inhibited by the insects activities.

Mrs. Allen enjoyed the Park Road house garden and art, "though there was not much time for leisure with a small child." Having moved to Park Road, it was in the same vicinity where her Grandfather and Great Aunt had lived. The Allen family joined the Congregational Church in Park Road when the Revd. T. J. Lander was minister.

FRUIT QUEUES

Mrs. Reynolds like many other newly married women in 1953 liked the fashionable shopping baskets of the time. "Rationing" she wrote "hadn't finished. So if you saw somebody with bananas you would ask if they had them from Rose's or Chamberlain's, then go to the appropriate fruiterers." Joan "like most couples mixed up butter and marg together and when you ran out of sugar, used condensed milk in your tea." Other queues that came to mind were at "Pop Wright's sweet shop and at Woolworths for chocolate biscuits."

BI-DIRECTIONAL INDICATORS

The Gumbleys had a Morris 8 - 'DOK 11', with full length running boards, spare wheel mounted on the back and those mechanical indicators. David wrote "My dad was once coming from Erdington and on reaching the cross roads at the Yenton, indicated left. Both indicators came out and the policeman on duty came up to the car, scratched his head and asked "Which way are you going?" Another time at the Yenton "Dad drove through the roundabout on the tram tracks in the fog and had a lucky escape."

CELEBRITY CHOICE

Birmingham shops continually challenged for Suttonians' shopping money and it was frequently mentioned that the Borough's wide selection of shops offered a personal service to customers that was not always available in the large, busy city stores. Birmingham firms aggressively refuted such a slur. Like many shop staff, Harold Groves "particularly enjoyed meeting the customers" at Chamberlain's Sutton Parade and Boldmere shops. There could be some disruption in the queues when certain customers "would wait to be served by Harold." In later years, one well-known Midland celebrity, A.T.V. presenter Jean Morton, always waited until her favourite staff member, Harold, was free to serve her. Mr. Groves's son, Wesley, noted "Harold's strong Christian principles would not allow him to sell bad products to anyone or to give short change or short weight." These principles may have influenced customers to prefer his service, but it also enhanced Chamberlain's name "for honest quality."

PROPOSED RAILWAY HALT

The showing of the 'Titfield Thunderbolt' at the Odeon gave the Railway Development Association the opening to arrange an exhibition in the cinema foyer about their activities. Considerable interest was received over the R.D.A. model of a simple halt which "the Association feels could be used at Coles Lane, Maney" on the old Midland Railway route that linked Wolverhampton and Birmingham New Street via Walsall, Aldridge, Streetly, Sutton Park, Walmley, Castle Bromwich and Saltley.

ABERCROMBIE PLAN ACHIEVABLE

Sutton news column writer Freres informed readers that "one thing that strikes me in particular, when travelling around the District, is the large number of new houses being erected in the Borough." He had little doubt that the Abercrombie plan estimate of a 70,000 population for the Town would be attained. Not surprisingly, he thought the "greatest housing development taking place was the Falcon Lodge Estate." The Council's decision that, in the near future, all further construction of Corporation housing would be on this estate supported this view. Freres spoke of the Springfield Estate where private houses were being constructed nearer to Walmley village.

The re-routing of the London-Liverpool road, one of the four main roads planned to link various parts of the country, would cut through the northeast corner of the Falcon Lodge Estate. The new road would incorporate part of the Sutton by-pass, plans of which had been drawn up before the War, and divert traffic away from the town centre onto the new A38.

BOROUGH ENGINEER'S DEPARTMENT

Stuart Mustow in the Sutton Coldfield Borough Engineer's Department "was involved in the resurfacing of Springfield Road." He informed me that it was not an easy job because it had to be "specially cambered with a large number of gullies." According to Mr. Mustow, Sutton Park had a strong attraction for the engineers. The engineers had the use of blue Ford vans and "always aimed at running through the Park wherever the job was!" Stuart recalled some interesting characters in the Department. John Porter, the Borough Engineer, "was a tall, quietly spoken, polite man who was thinning on top." Henry Higgs, as Chief Clerk, "knew the ropes better than anyone" and was also known for being "a lively, sparky chap." The Chief Assistant was "Arthur Spencer, a train and tram buff, who was a good engineer, a committed Christian and a reader at Boldmere Parish Church."

The Borough's Building Inspector was John Bennett who had previously worked in the Colonies. "He was a larger than life character, if ever there was one!" Brian Webb and Roy Hudson were former officers from the forces and "Fred Green was a quiet, but effective engineer."

END OF TRAM LINE

The final day of the City of Birmingham Tram Operations, including the No.2 route to Chester road Tram Terminus, was on Saturday, 4th July, 1953. Dr. John Raines' picture on that last day shows the service number as 60 which was incorrect as it should have been No.2. To the left of tram 597 is the time-clock. Across the Sutton Road is a bus stop for the 64 bus service which was due to start the next day. John commented "The trams were very high vehicles in proportion to their width and a

A City of Birmingham No.2. Tram service, masquerading as a No. 60. Service, on the last day of operation at Chester Road Tram Terminus on 4th. July 1953. (Dr. J. Raines)

ride down Gravelly Hill in the upper saloon was quite a hair raising experience – not recommended to those of a nervous disposition!" John remembered the "uncomfortable wooden seats. The back-rest consisted of a single horizontal piece of wood which could be moved backwards or forwards so that passengers could face the direction of travel." Incidentally, some of the seats later found use at Sutton Coldfield C.C.'s ground as seating for spectators at Rectory Park.

DECLINING BUS PASSENGERS

Perhaps, not only did a Sutton Councillor find out that Suttonians paid the highest bus fares in the country, but also other Midland 'Red' passengers felt the same and stopped using the buses. The 48th A.G.M. of the Midland 'Red' Bus Company learnt that, for the first time in many years, the number of passengers showed a decline. The earlier declaration from a M.'R'. spokesperson that the railways were more vulnerable than buses to the use of private cars needed to be reconsidered at least on the 1862 railway line. The News continued "the new Transport Act had become law giving a decent burial to area schemes for nationalisation" which had so long threatened M.'R'. activities. The element of "healthy road and rail competition is maintained in the Midlands."

CANWELL BABY HOSPITAL

The Canwell Baby Hospital opened in 1931. Susie King the Night Superintendent at the hospital from 1938 – 1953 said "It was the first specialist hospital for babies, part of a national plan for regional provision throughout the United Kingdom" it closed in the spring 1953. The patients and nursing staff had been transferred to the Little Bromwich Hospital's new children unit.

An official of the Selly Oak Hospital Group under whose jurisdiction Canwell Hospital came told the News, "that no decision had been made on the future use of the hospital, which would be a matter for the Midland Regional Board to decide."

After children and staff had been transferred following the official closure, Susie and resident maid Doris Redfern remained and set about cataloguing all the hospitals contents "down to every item of linen." The two staff had a real concern about the security over such a large rambling establishment, including the old monastery cells.

A man who worked at Good Hope was employed at night as the regular watchman. In an effort to reduce their apprehension Susie and Doris left many lights on throughout the building during the night. Eventually the inventory was completed, releasing the two ladies. Miss King became Matron of St. Editha's in Tamworth.

The earlier details about the Canwell Baby Hospital are in pages 13–14, 46–47, Sutton Coldfield in the Forties, Brewin Books, 2003.

SUTTON AND DISTRICT CORONATION CELEBRATIONS

Street group correspondents and Sutton Coldfield News reporters recorded some of the "thousand-and-one celebrations, which were held in every corner of the Borough and district on Coronation Day and week". Although the Canwell Baby Hospital had closed, Babies were in sharp focus in Walmley's programme of "Something for everyone." Despite rain and a biting wind, about 2,000 visited Penns park, where a baby show was held in a small marquee. Dr. C. Ramsdale's selection as the champion baby was six month old, Philip Brough.

The Sutton News considered the proudest Suttonian on Coronation Day was eight year old peter Richardson of New Oscott, who shared the same day for his birthday with the Queen. "What's more," the reporter commented, "they had exchanged letters on the subject, with Peter getting a prompt reply to his letter."

A nine year old Grange Lane boy had mixed feelings about his London visit for the Coronation. Waiting at a Blackheath bus stop, a wheel flew off a passing lorry, causing injuries to David Pugh, necessitating treatment in a London Hospital.

POPULAR ALTERNATIVE TO ORGANIZED ACTIVITIES

A survey of Wylde Green, Boldmere and New Oscott spoke of "residents mainly spent Coronation day quietly, with a few street parties." An absence of traffic on the roads and the emptiness of the streets implied, "obviously, most people spent the day quietly watching T.V. coverage." Although many individual houses were well and tastefully decorated, "for the majority, most occupants did not bother." A correspondent summed it up, "there was a paucity of decorations in these three districts." The laid-back approach to the celebrations in the area was also noted at the Princess Alice School, where the one hundred and sixty children "spent most of the day watching television on one of the six T.V. sets in the school, with members of the staff or friends outside." Because of the poor weather, tea was held in the school. After sports in the grounds, "everyone went back to watching T.V. in the evening."

Coronation Display. Mrs. Shelia Crockett's display in her Ebrook Road/Jerome Road shop front. (Mrs. Shelia Crockett)

A disappointment for many in the town was the cancellation of the Coronation Day carnival because of insufficient entries, but the Coronation Regatta on Saturday 6th July, on Powell's pool was successful. The crowd of several hundreds enjoyed a packed afternoon of aquatic events. The Coronation Ball attended by about four hundred in the Town Hall was also a success.

David Wilkins like many other youngsters had their coronation arrangements swiftly changed owing to the rain. Because it "was a wet day, our Jerome Road Coronation Party was held in the Sutton Town football club social building of concrete and corrugated iron." He sang "How much is that 'Doggie in the window' for an extra tub of ice cream!"

There was also a party for schools in the Orange Grove with the use of Pat Collins fun fair. There was a pageant on the Meadow Platt. "We had tea and free rides" David added.

TRIPS OVER THE BOUNDARY

At least three local celebrations included a peep into the city of Birmingham festivities. The Coronation Day highlight for ninety children from Elizabeth Road during the afternoon was a "coach trip round Birmingham to see the decorations. Each child received a souvenir Coronation Bible or a fountain pen set." Three coaches of old people were equally entertained by the Whitehouse Common organizers, with an excursion around Birmingham Coronation decorations, plus each participant given a monetary gift. Riland Road "old folks went to see other decorations and celebration in the area by coach."

Sports were on the agenda for most of the street or district parties, though the inclement weather forced the Kineton and Welford roads sports to be transferred to Britwell Hall "at the last minute." The alternative provision involved a 'taxi' service of private cars to transport two hundred and fifty, adults and children. George Road, welcomed the Mayor and Mayoress who distributed five shilling pieces to more than fifty children. The road claimed to possibly have had the "most varied programme of events in the Borough that day." The largest Coronation Cake mentioned in reports was the Reddicap Hill and Coleshill road one at twenty eight pounds, sampled by the sixty children plus adults in the Coleshill Road scout hut, following the sports and fancy dress parade. Fancy dress was one of the most popular events at the Coles lane-Lower end rescheduled Maney Church Hall location. Food for nearly one hundred children and two hundred adults had been prepared. The Farthing Lane party included a fancy dress parade with an after tea Punch and Judy show. Before the bonfire and fireworks there was a distribution of souvenirs.

A presentation to the Guest of Honour during the Riland Road children's fancy dress competition. (Bernard R. Haynes)

BEST DECORATED HOUSE

Before the Riland Road children's sports in Rectory park was transferred to Victoria Road Schools, Mr. and Mrs. Rushworth were declared winner's of the road's best decorated house.

A similar award won on the Falcon lodge Estate was by Mr. Hunt of Rectory Road. There were highly recommended houses in, Chadwick Road, Reddicap Heath Road, Newdigate Road, Churchill Road and Cattell Drive.

Concern for others was apparent at a number of the celebrations. Food parcels and flowers were taken by Whitehouse Common workers to eighteen bedridden invalids in the district. The Streetly activities began on the Sunday with the unveiling of a plaque on the war memorial in the grounds of All Saints Church, in the memory of eleven Streetly servicemen who gave their lives in W.W.II.

FAIRY AVENUE

That was the description to lighting in the main gate area to the Park. "Colour lights were suspended from tree to tree along Park Road from the junction with Upper Clifton Road and Clifton Road." The lighting was extended in a similar manner

John Cooper's coronation event in Rectory park caught the attention of children and adults. Mr. Cooper lived in Riland Grove. He was a registered Football Association referee. (Bernard R. Haynes)

along the road into the Park. "The pay boxes were outlined in colour electric lights, and decorated with the Tudor Rose."

The Town's firework display in the Park was presented by Wilder Fireworks, providing "a great spectacle for those who braved the weather to the end." Several fascinating mounted pieces included a "100' shower, imitating Niagara Falls. The display closed with portrayals of the Queen and Duke of Edinburgh, with the words 'God bless them.' The bonfire had been erected by Park staff with brushwood and deadwood.

SUTTON - SECOND TO NONE

The superiority of sporting ability in one area of the Borough's Schools was evident at the coronation inter-schools sports arranged by the local Athletic Association, held in Sutton Park. The three thousand crowd saw the Boldmere County Schools win five out of the six trophies.

As part of the grand Finale to the Town's celebrations the Four Oaks parade was led by its own band. Three hundred children dressed in a variety of costumes, paraded around the district to the Riding Schools Fields in Clarence Road. The

Councillor and Mrs. Woodcock had not expected to meet celebrity Charlie Chaplin (Mrs. Rose Pearson), at the Holland Road Playing Fields Coronation Party. (J & D Kirkman /Mrs. L. Hunt)

evening entertainment was a puppet show, ventriloquist, and community singing. Chronically sick children were sent food parcels.

WORLDS BEST WATER SUPPLY

The News made the bold statement that throughout the recorded history of the Royal Town that Suttonians stand "second to none in the Realm in their loyalty to the throne."

About the time of the Coronation the U.K. Water Companies Association also entered the boasting stakes. Britain they claimed had the best water supply in the World. "More than 95% of the population enjoys a piped supply of pure water, at the cost of a few pence a week."

DECREASING SCHOOL POPULATION

The proposed new secondary modern school in the Borough "was a long way off" according to the Education officer. He anticipated the "School population would probably be decreasing not increasing The births were: 1947, 857; 1948, 743; 1949, 654; 1951, 636; with approximately 560 in 1952. A number of extensions however had been included in an emergency classroom programme for 1953-54.

MANORISMS

Mr. & Mrs. Woodcock's daughter, Valerie was asked to provide entertainment at the Manor Operatic Society's Dinner. The Manorisms was her answer, being a selected group from the parent company. There were six gents, bass and tenor, including Valerie's father, and six being sopranos and contraltos and three dancers. Mrs. Woodcock as the group's dresser, had the men like the Black and White minstrals, dressed alike. They did not black their faces. The ladies wore pretty afternoon dresses. Valerie made special movements for the group, and they sang in harmony, all the popular songs. After the interval the men changed into evening dress and the ladies likewise. The successful performances were followed by "bookings at the Town Hall; Belfrey; Top Rank, Birmingham and many other organizations." The Manorisms were a great success. A little was taken for expenses the rest of the donations "went towards the welfare of elderly people in the town."

HIGHBRIDGE ROAD RESCUES

(Left) Highbridge Road Rescues. Miss Hudson sent a pictorial record of the local scouts providing an alternative transport and rescue service when Highbridge Road was partially closed because of flooding. The scout, powered wagon enabled shoppers and travellers to get home without getting their purchases and selves wet. Presumably it was Bob-a-Job plus! (Miss A. S. Hudson)

(Right) On another occasion a Northern Ireland Railway vehicle requiring a safe route, Pickfords followed the scout's example and travelled along Highbridge Road. (Miss A. S. Hudson)

ORCHESTRA SAVED FROM COLLAPSE

A healthy and growing sport was encouraged by the Council's Park and Estate committee, with a plot of land, dedicated to its promotion in Rectory Park. There was no danger to the community or club membership. The Council considered the new Archery Club in the Borough with nine members had good prospects for succeeding.

Council intervention with help from the rates avoided the collapse of the Sutton Coldfield Symphony Orchestra. During the 1952/53 season seven works not previously played in the town were included in four concerts, enabling the Society to claim "they kept abreast of the times," and "probably gave better value for money than any other symphonic society." Sutton was not afraid of claiming leadership in many areas of life. Mr. Harold Gray, the respected musician, was the Orchestra's Musical Director. The impression was given the season's programme and leadership resulted in the highest Society membership in their history being achieved.

SMALL INVESTOR'S SCHEME

The 1952 introduced small investors loan scheme from sources other than the public works loan Board was attracting a steady flow of offers particularly from "local small investors." The outside sources loans totalled £70,000.

Council members were concerned about the loans from the Public Works Loan Board, mainly in respect of housing development, which as the Town's largest bill, exceeded £2m. It would have to be repaid by 2010, with interest.

CORPORATION HOUSE SALES

Six Corporation house tenants had positively responded to the leaflet distributed to all Sutton Council house tenants offering the opportunity to buy their council property. Apparently no offers had been received on post-war houses, only on pre-war homes.

RELIEF AT BLAKE STREET

Having reached the age of eighteen, my junior porter status was replaced by one of an adult porter and subsequent adult pay. Four Oaks had no establishment for adult porters, so relief porter positions came my way, as the inevitable call-up date drew closer. I cannot recall visiting Blake Street Station before I arrived one morning for the early turn, at the country location. Once past Four Oaks, the Blake Street – Lichfield city and Trent Valley service was sparse with regular gaps of two – three hours. Small as it was Blake Street had a busy goods yard with weighbridge and on site coal merchants. Forgotten by many, on the upside stood a signal box operated

Few folk using Blake Street station these days could visualize this 1956 shot of the wooden planked platforms with oil lamps and portable steps. It was the same when the author was on relief duties there. (E. S. Russell)

each working day as required. The ancient water supply came from the station manually worked pump, complemented by oil lamps and low wooden planked platforms, with portable steps. Sitting on the platform seats in the summer of 1953, the staff and passengers were in the country, with few houses around. Yet, they were overshadowed by the towering seven hundred and fifty foot T.V. transmitter, opened in December, 1949. Even so I have no memories of the mast being intrusive, some how it had become a generally accepted part of the environment. Though in August, 1953, the mast again became a news item in the local paper.

Blake Street station was important for passengers living in hamlets, isolated farms, Little Hay and Stonall. Sutton park's first signalwoman in 1942, and the first on the L.M.S., Eileen Kirkham, was a Stonall woman. Blake Street had ten weekday services, the first up train to Birmingham left at 6.38a.m. arriving at New Street at 7.20a.m. Local people who needed to be in the City before 7.00a.m., had the couple of miles to walk, a cycle ride, or car parking at Four Oaks, to go on the 6.10a.m. On the down line deeper into Staffordshire, the first service at 7.04a.m. arrived at Lichfield City at 7.17a.m. with an ex-Walsall train connection, arriving at the Trent Valley station at 7.43a.m. Regular passengers knew the Blake Street staff so were inquisitive to find out why I was there, but willing to put me right over the local fares and train times.

PARCELS MUST GET THROUGH

In the relative quiet of Four Oaks station car park and encouragement from Tom Compton, Mr. Shallis and Mr. Webb, I learnt to ride a cycle and gained confidence to ride around the car park. My confidence however, did not stand-up to a task required of Blake Street staff. A large parcel waiting delivery to a Little Hay farm, caused me much anxiety. The cost of sending the parcel by rail included the delivery to the isolated farm. I tried to ride the heavy old station cycle with parcel rack on the front, but kept coming to grief. Much to the amusement of Blake Street and Little Hay residents I pushed the heavy cycle with the parcel up to the A38, over the cross roads and down to the farm, out of breath and highly embarrassed. At least it got there – undamaged. The 1884 built station seemed to have changed little in it's almost seventy years of existence, in 1953. There were probably few, if any, Blake Street and area residents who could have visualized the dramatic change to their environment, some years later. There became a need for another station between Blake Street and Four Oaks opened in 1957, which was a surprise for some.

Blake Street was a station, where I was the sole person on duty, whereas at Four Oaks there was always someone, even from another department nearby. Though the signal box and weighbridge were staffed when I was on duty, some how, there was no contact.

VILLAGE STATION ATTRACTION

My hours of searching through the national time table at Four oaks, to learn about railway services in the West Midlands and beyond, paid off when on relief work, without the booking Clerk's and Station Master around. In the summer of 1953, even with the increase of car ownership, train and coach holiday traffic remained popular. Folk would arrive at rural stations asking for time's, fares, probably having found suitable accommodation advertised in the Holiday Haunts guide. In those days, far more holiday destinations, including many on the coast, were accessible by rail. Similar to car ownership, more people had telephones, but for millions, the hamlet or village telephone Kiosk was their phone link. In an emergency a phone connected business neighbour, or farmer may be willing to help, if the kiosk phone was out of order.

The deciding on where to go for the holiday, working out of the alternative railway routes, comparing journey times, number of changes, left luggage facilities, were part of the adventure for the many once or twice a year long distance rail travellers. For those railway passengers to chat over the arrangements at their local, generally friendly station, where they knew the two or three regular staff members, made it a worthwhile, attractive and pleasant experience.

The booking of a long distance rail journey to Penzance, Scarborough, Llandudno, Hunstanton, Ilfracombe, Edinburgh, Oban or Dublin for two or more, certainly enhanced the monthly ticket sales for little stations like Blake Street. Generally, relief station personnel who knew the necessary information, or could look it up in a reasonable time, were gradually accepted by the local population. They trusted them to arrange advanced collection and delivery of luggage and insurance cover, being further revenue for the quiet often isolated station. Although in a new environment for me with a limited train service all trains were met, tickets collected, assistance given, and trains safely sent away. There was usually time for a few friendly remarks as the same train staff, seen at Four oaks, worked the trains through Blake Street. Help with prams, pushchairs, and luggage for those willing to use the many stairs at Blake Street, was available, helping to build up good customer care relations. In those days, the care and support of passengers was expected, whether the Station Master was about or not!

FREIGHT TRAIN
The week day freight train tripper, No. 162 left Curzon Street at 9.10am. arriving, after numerous shunting and marshalling arrives down the Sutton branch at Blake Street by 12.24p.m. later it went onto Shenstone, leaving at 2.50p.m. due to cover

Freight facilities. This rare view of Blake Street weighbridge and storage facilities to the south of the station remained in the country. (Mike Lewis)

the 2½ miles back to Blake Street against the gradient in 10 minutes. Fifteen minutes was allowed for further shunting, and truck collections, then onto Four Oaks for another fifteen minutes, forty seven minutes at Sutton Coldfield and ten at Erdington. I regret not recording more of the activities of Blake Street.

ARMY PREFERENCE

Someone informed me a railway employee's manager could write to the army authorities, recommending the service recruit be placed at the Royal Engineers Railway Transport Unit at Longmoor Military Railway in Hampshire. Mr. Shallis made some enquiries, finding out the various trades and types of jobs offered. Working on a railway with staff from various occupations, sharing a common commitment to the use of railways was attractive to me. Although the R.E.'s in the Railway Transport Unit would have to be trained in the use of arms, the anticipated day to day activities would not normally be involved with firing rifles. It was understood the operating of the railways in war theatres could be highly dangerous with trains extremely vulnerable, as mentioned in Sutton Coldfield in the Forties.[1]

Mr. Shallis went through the list of occupations available. A number were not appropriate to me, because of a lack of training and qualifications. We eventually came down to engine cleaning, locomotive fireman and permanent way track layer/lengthman. The Four Oaks Station master recommended the locomotive fireman or track layer/lengthman grades were within my capabilities and ones I wanted to do. So off went the letter that held many of my future service hopes with it.

FURTHER DOWN THE LINE

Apart from Blake Street the only other station I went to relieve at, was on the former 1849 South Staffordshire Railway's, Alrewas Station, the first stop after Lichfield Trent Valley. Travelling on the first weekday train to Lichfield City, with a change there, I arrived at Alrewas at 7.59a.m. It took another seven minutes to Barton and Walton, reaching Burton–upon-Trent at 8.15a.m. Alrewas station in 1953 offered seven weekday trains to Burton and six to Lichfield City, including a Derby-Birmingham via Sutton Coldfield train. The same trunk road that travelled through Sutton Parade, later crossing over the railway bridge at Four Oaks, the A38, ran along the edge of Alrewas, with almost all of the village on the side away from the station, which was on the Tamworth road. Gerald known as Gel, Dollin worked for six months at Alrewas station, when he was 21, but moved when his duties included maintaining signal lamps on the Midland main line. He did not like heights, something I had to deal with after my stint of National Service. Mr. Dollin transferred in 1952 to Lichfield

---

1. *Sutton Coldfield in the Forties, Brewin Books 2003 p.12.*

City Goods department as a goods checker. According to Gel when I was relieving at Alrewas the complement of staff was a Station Master/Goods Agent, two station porters, and a goods checker. On reflection, I expect the Station Master made me aware of my duties, which keys fitted where, the cash balance, most popular tickets, parcels etc. Surprisingly I have no recollection of inservice training by anybody.

One of the first of the early turn porter's duties was the lighting of four oil lamps on the Burton side platform. This was difficult to achieve as could be imagined in windy conditions. There were two Aladdin lamps, one in the booking office and one in the booking hall/waiting room. As my relief work was in the summer, those duties were not appropriate, though they would probably need maintaining on the morning turn. Similar to Four Oaks and Blake Street, the early porter lit the fires, when needed. Having opened the station, and checked the one pound balance, and closing ticket numbers from the previous operating day, the booking hall window was pulled open.

Some of the Burton and Derby bound travellers were railway people, including footplate staff at Burton, such as Ronny Lindsey, though he and colleagues on pre-passenger train services, hitched a lift on a passing light engine. There was a solitary lamp on the Lichfield side with an open type waiting shelter. Passengers waiting for Lichfield services in cold or wet weather were known to keep warm and dry in the main building, until the crossing gates were closed and signals set for the train on the far side.

R.A.F. IMPORTS

Haunton Hall Nunnery brought Alrewas, much trunk collection and delivery business. Being a silent order, the railway staff, like other outsiders, could only communicate with the one Hall member, authorized to speak, when they had to visit the hall. An Off-Licence in the Main Street, "sold a bit of everything:" Gel told me, "being open all hours." In bad weather, such as thick fog around the Trent valley with later running trains the porter's could be handed a box with a budgerigar or parrot on the last service from Burton-upon-Trent.

Sometimes at 11p.m. Mr. Dollin put the basket on the station cycle, taking it into the village to Johann Dickinson's shop for his own collection of livestock with the receipt of acceptance, Gel happily returned to Alrewas station, having earned half an hour's overtime. Other livestock found at the station, were cats. Gerald's sister took her son to see the station 'kittens'. The Railway allocated 5/- a month to feed the cats, which only lasted a week. An older cat caught and ate 27 mice in one day! That particular feline was more productive in vermin arrest than the rodent controller from Walsall, in Mr. Dollin's estimation.

It would be interesting to learn from R.A.F. Fradley cooks what was the favourite meal on the camp during the 1950s, because a probable contender was frequently handled by Alrewas railway staff. Four boxes arrived by passenger train then taken up to the camp by a B.R. lorry driver from Lichfield, at regular intervals. Gel described the four or so boxes as they defrosted, omitting a dreadful smell, with recently congealed blood seeping out. Each box was full of Australian skinned rabbits for the local R.A.F. The state of the dead animals on arrival at Alrewas made the railway staff think twice before they ate rabbit dishes.

FISH AND FLOWERS
Other boxes that needed prompt delivery after arrival by passenger train were those containing fresh fish. The stench in the guard's compartment and area on the platform lingered for hours. The railway van took them over to "the Tofts at the Tree Café, with the fish being fried with chips and sold from a van in the village and hamlets around Alrewas." Apparently it was an appreciated and anticipated community service, reaching homes that with limited transport otherwise would have been denied a relativity inexpensive and stable diet at the time.

The railway van regularly called at a local address for consignments that needed fast conveyance to be available for sale next morning. Wychnor Flowers grew a large variety of flowers including Gladioli. The lovely blooms were processed through Alrewas station, with an eye on the next train to Lichfield Trent Valley, then forwarded to London for the market, by a fast service. If the flowers were in danger

Alrewas Station Staff had a selection of consignments to deal with. (Mike Lewis)

of missing the London connection the van driver took them direct to the T.V. railway station. The release of pigeons on practice flights, and onto contests, saw a number of baskets at the rural station.

GOODS CHECKER

It seemed to have been a pleasant experience at Alrewas. Gradually I became familiar with the station duties. One Saturday, a railway family came to the booking window for privilege tickets to Burton. Looking in the draws and cupboards I could not find the correct quarter fares, so worked out the cost from prices available to me. As the family did not complain, the fares they paid may have been less than normal!

Gerald returned to Alrewas in 1954 as their goods checker. He worked closely with the Station master, and the local based coal merchant and his half-brother mate, Tommy Payne. Mr. Orme, the owner of Alrewas Mills, had 1,000 tons of fertilizer at intervals delivered in fifty, ten ton wagons. Because of limited accommodation, a restricted number went in the yard, the rest put in the siding. So influential was Mr. Orme in the community, he was regularly called 'Sir' by service providers and meant.

CROSSING PATROL OFFICERS

With less than a month before my civilian freedom was to be wrenched away, subjects of local Sutton concern included the introduction of crossing patrol officers. There was growing apprehension over the rising national road casualty rate of children, particularly with going and returning from school. The motorists and other road users were concerned of the long lines of traffic built up, when just two or three children crossed. Sutton brought in a voluntary system of crossing patrol officers shepherding children across roads, with 'stop' notices. A Government Bill was in the process of preparation, to authorise the employment of patrols.

Motorists were advised in the town to make themselves aware of the recently introduced signs prohibiting parking on the approach to pedestrian crossings. Sutton Coldfield was one of the Boroughs in the West Midlands to adopt the new regulations similar to, Cannock and Wolverhampton. Three motorists found guilty of waiting in prohibited area on the approach side of pedestrian crossings in Sutton, were given absolute discharge. The court however, warned motorists those decisions should not be regarded as "a precedent in any shape or form." Local shopkeepers protested they were losing trade through the "present restrictions on parking facilities in Sutton Coldfield."

KEEP ON WALKING

A Saturday evening radio commentary in July emphasised Sutton Coldfield Walking and Athletic Club's D. Carter's one mile junior championship walk when he beat the previous three year record by 22 seconds. Another Sutton member, G. Hall, came forth in a twenty four hour race in Motspur Park, Surrey. He began the walk steadily on Friday night, increasing to a speed, as he progressed. The race was over 105 miles 440 yards. During the long, arduous contest he received expert support and attention by S.C.W.A.C. members. J.T. MacDonnell and T. Billingham.

DESERT OF PAPER

With my mind more anxiously fixed on joining up day, the August Bank Holiday Monday paid attendance equalled the record of 1948 with 38,017, passed me by. British Rail ran a shuttle service and the Midland 'Red' augmented their Main Road and Perry Barr services. Park Forester, T. J. Allen, advised Feres "the area around the main entrance to the park looked like a 'desert of paper.'" From the litter point of view, the park staff considered "the holiday had been a bad one."

YOU'RE NOT A 'MR', YOU'RE A SAPPER

Somehow the beautiful background of the Malvern Hills, from my Norton barracks, Worcester billet window did nothing to ease my sorrow of leaving proper life behind for two years in Her Majesties Service. The N.C.O.'s in that Royal Engineer's assessment camp made us raw recruits very much aware that we were no longer, 'Misters', we had become 'Sappers' for at least two years. The sensible one's amongst us we learnt, would sign on for a minimum of three years, as proper regular soldiers, with enhanced pay and opportunities. I had no trouble in not being enticed to become a regular, even on the lesser money.

The pervading smell that stayed with me for a long time from the Worcester camp was the mess room stench of margarine, it obliterated everything else, accompanied by plates of fatty inedible so called food. I certainly was in the Army now. In 1953-55 excerpts from National Service days will be included but the intention is to stay most of the time in or around Sutton Coldfield.

MAST OVERHAUL

After continuous service of three and a half years, the B.B.C.'s high power vision and sound transmitters at Sutton Coldfield, were taken out of service for an essential overhaul and some improvements. Standby medium power transmitters provided the service in the meanwhile, with weaker signals noticeable in outlying areas.

At the Sutton inquest on the death by drowning of a Birmingham man in Keepers Pool, during the bank holiday, the Coroner acknowledged there were seven staff supervising the swimming. However he thought, "they are no good on the bank. At bank Holiday times it does seem there is a need for an extra boat there."

STATION OFFICER'S HOME CALL

An Officer-in-charge from Sutton Fire Station with appliance squad, responded to a '999' call in Walmley Ash Road, after a Chipmunk Trainer from Castle Bromwich Aerodrome had crashed into his neighbour's bungalow. S.O. Whitton checking the bungalow, realised the Pilotless plane had also demolished part of his own bungalow. He told the News, "After the initial shock, it was just a normal job to me, and the whole thing is just an unfortunate occurrence." A twenty year old cadet from Kent, was on a ninety minute aerobatic flight as part of a fifteen day training course at Castle Bromwich. Having turned the aircraft upside down at 8,000 feet he was unable to right it. He baled out at 2,000 feet, landing in a fir tree at Birlec Sports ground, in Signal Hayes Road. The Groundsman assisted him down, then took him to the Castle Bromwich Aerodrome sick bay. The main damage was inflicted on Donald Whitton's neighbour's home.

FIREMAN'S TRAINING FOR LATER

Within a week of the Walmley accident, our local firemen were called out to another incident, this time a railway crash, working alongside colleagues from Tamworth and Atherstone fire stations. A Bradford-Bristol express train, carrying three hundred and sixty six passengers was derailed in a cutting between Tamworth and Kingsbury, with one passenger taken to hospital. The derailment resulted in the train splitting into two parts. The locomotive overturned on its side and the first coach flung across the rails. The remaining seven coaches left the track, toppling over against an embankment. The Sutton fireman's main task, that kept them busy throughout the early hours, was filling the ballast on the cranes that lifted the engine and coaches. They also generally assisted with the removal of debris. That type of experience at a railway crash site may have provided some Sutton Fire and rescue personnel valuable knowledge for a internationally recorded emergency, seventeen months later.

AMMUNITION HOARDERS

Parents of some Streetly children were extremely anxious to learn their off-springs had located and secretly hoarded live ammunition from the first world war at their popular playground, near Chester Road North. The News understood the rounds of live ammunition had been dumped at unmarked locations from the W.W.I. Birmingham Ammunition Company. However through soil erosion over the years the "ammunition is being revealed and hundreds of rounds can be easily seen." The wooded area belonged to a Birmingham businessman who agreed with Staffordshire Police, to fence off the forty five acres, and erect danger notices.

1950 BUSINESS

In 1953, details emerged that the town's four hundred and forty retail shops in 1950 had total sales of £4,349,000, employing one thousand, four hundred and forty seven full time and four hundred and seventy eight part time staff. Their total earnings being £330,000. The survey comparing Sutton Coldfield and Solihull showed:

	1950 population	Retail Shops	Sales
Sutton Coldfield	47,400	440	£4,349,000
Solihull	67,640	496	£4,340,000

Mr. N. Howes, joint secretary of Sutton Coldfield Chamber of Trade, recognising the figures were three years out of date, felt "to make comparisons on a population basis alone was wrong, for the amenities of the town attract people from the surrounding areas."

Six or seven Beeches Walk shops began an experiment, for the benefit of "business people returning from the city." They remained open on Friday's until 7p.m. Mr. R. Broad of the Beeches Walk Travel and Hardware Store was one of the organizers.

FALCON LODGE POOL FILLED IN

Probably with memories of the Bank holiday drowning at Keepers Pool, the Falcon lodge Residents Association sought the assistance of the Town Council to eliminate such potential incidents on the estate. The request for action originated from complaints by residents that the pool at the rear of St. Chad's Road was a considerable danger to children on Falcon lodge. Parental anxieties focused on the danger of disease and infection from the stagnant pool. The Borough Surveyor later informed the F.L.R.A. the owner had agreed to the pool being filled in.

Freres revealed the Revd. David Loake, was to take charge of the Falcon Lodge estate on behalf of the Church-of-England.

WORRYING NEW HOUSING TREND

Sutton Coldfield's Medical Officer of Health's 1952 report highlighted a housing trend that troubled him. He reported "Many of the larger houses in certain areas of the town are being let room by room, and the occupants have few, if any, facilities or amenities." At the time there were no local byelaws to govern the situation in the town. He expressed an urgent need for newly made byelaws to be issued and the sooner the opportunity "given to this Corporation of studying them, the better it will be."

Local police were aware of offside parking, with the car displaying the obligatory lights facing vehicles approaching on their nearside. An early offender in Park Drive was fined £2 by the local bench.

TOWN NOT CONSULTED

The town Council was alerted to the Warwickshire County Council plan under which the Borough would take 24,000 of Birmingham's overspill in the next 20 years. Coun. W. F. Taylor, Chairman of the General Purposes Committee told the October Town Council meeting that the Council was not invited to the discussions. However the C.C. had discussed proposals with Worcestershire, Staffordshire and Birmingham City. At an informal discussion with the town's home county, certain members of the Sutton Council, "could not see its way to accept" the proposals.

The only viable solution that the Sutton Committee saw for the over-spill problem "was the building of a new town and transporting both industry and people to that new town." Sutton's current annual population was increasing by a thousand. It would have been far greater for the Council, than anticipated except for the restrictions on building following the war.

HELICOPTER ROTOR - STATION

A separate local central area development plan for 1968-1973 by Sutton Council had designed to alleviate traffic and parking problems, including a major project of a by-pass of the Parade. Councillor H. H. Turner, Chairman of the Highways Committee welcomed the building of a by-pass, parallel with the Parade. It would extend the town laterally instead of "stretching along one main street, as at present." The by-pass would entail "large-scale demolition of the east side. The borough Surveyor told the News the main objection to the plan would include "additional parking facilities and shopping areas."

The plan also provided for 11 blocks of shops, about 12 blocks of flats, surrounded by open spaces and trees, 4 blocks of offices, 2 hotels, and a health centre. Quite a forward thinking innovation was to be a Helicopter Rotor Station sited between Avenue Road and the railway embankment.

Birmingham's overspill problems were vigorously discussed at a subsequent meeting with W.C.C., when a Sutton Alderman described the nearby City as a "gigantic octopus." He begged the County Authority "to exercise the utmost care to see we do not get into the grasp of its (Birmingham's) withering tentacles." The Sutton spokesman feared the town and Solihull would be swallowed up as Erdington and Handsworth had been in the past. Both towns, "were straining to take people from Birmingham's overcrowded lodging houses." Apparently, 75% of Sutton Coldfield's post-war houses were occupied by people who worked in the city.

NEW CAR PRICES

In the 'News' Motor Show supplement some of the more affordable cars were listed, all included purchase tax: Ford Popular £390.14.5d; Austin 30 (2 door) £475.14.2d;

Ford Anglia £511.2.6d; Morris Minor (2 door) £529.10.10d; Ford Prefect £560.14.2d; Citron 2 c.v. £564.14.2d; Morris Minor Travellers car £599.13.4d. The dearest on the show list was the Bentley Continental at £6,928.12.6d, again including P.T.

A.A. DEVELOPMENTS

According to A.A. Patrolman Geoff Dixon the motor cycles used by them were B.S.A. M20, later using the M21 with the new telescopic forks. Inspectors used Triumph twin cylinder models (Speedtwin). During the twenty years Mr. Dixon was with the A.A. the machines and sidecars with leg shields, had windscreens. The actual sidecar boxes changed from metal, to a more streamlined fibreglass version.

Radio's, Geoff advised, me had been used on the Land Rovers for some time, and was obviously useful to the member who could telephone and have a vehicle directed to him. "The fitting of radio's to a few motor cycle sidecars were introduced in various areas of the country in about 1954 as an experiment. We were part of this in the Birmingham area." The disadvantage that the patrol staff experienced was when they were "just about to sign off for the evening at 7.00p.m. you were directed to another job because no one else was available."

R.A.F. 216 M.U. W.R.A.F.S

Mr. Graham's picture shows the W.R.A.F. at ease on the Whitehouse Common parade ground with some of the units facilities behind them. (Keith Graham)

Three members of the R.A.F. 216 M.U. Police close to Carhampton Road, and the maintenance centre in the rear. Corporal Hives is on the right. (Godfrey P. Hives)

R.A.F. POLICE
Another side of life at the Sutton R.A.F. station in post W.W.II days, is shared by corporal Godfrey Hives, as a member of the unit's police force. His tasks included Guard House duties, checking all personnel and loads in and out of the camp. He was also involved with court martials, following up of stealing of R.A.F. equipment from camp, and airmen and airwomen being improperly dressed.

The R.A.F. police had 3 cells on the camp. He particularly commented on the very good food together with the "facilities for cricket, football and tennis." Godfrey served at 216 M.U. between 1952-55.

T.V. CHIMPS AT SCHOOL
Gerry Taylor remembered Molly Badham and the T.V. Chimps that used to be in her pet shop. Miss Badham, Gerry wrote, "used to bring them to the Riland-Bedford school," to show, educate and entertain the children. The Chimps owner, "seemed a nice lady, and of course they later moved to Hints Zoo, a small pretty zoo on a hill, well before Twycross."

IMAGES MORE IMPORTANT THAN WORDS?
At another Sutton School, the headmistress questioned if a modern emphasis would replace the printed word. In her second annual report at the Sutton Coldfield High School for Girls, Miss M. Rothwell asked if the modern emphasis on picture images would be a preferred option to the printed word for the coming generation.

Form IV L, Sutton Coldfield High School for Girls, 1953, with Miss S. Davies, form mistress in the centre. (Julie Bishop)

U.N.A. APATHY
During a Town Forum in the Town Hall, arranged by the local branch of the United Nation's Association, one member in response to the reasons for public apathy towards the United Nations, "thought it was due to the fact that the U.N. was a similar organisation to the League of nation's." He continued, "People felt that the League was unable to prevent war, and the U.N. was equally likely to fail."

Betty Pitchford's new Walmley shop drew a large crowd, with the premises being "packed out." It was not too surprising, when the first 60 customers each received a free pair of nylons with their purchase!

ANTI-SMOG MASKS ON N.H.S.
On page 752 of The 20th Century Day by Day, D. K. 1999, in November 1953, Dr.'s were authorised to prescribe anti-smog masks for patients living in smoky areas and subject to heart or lung diseases. It may be Suttonians that worked long hours in Birmingham factories or out in the critical smog conditions, were prescribed the masks by their Sutton based G.P.'s.

1,700 PLUS BABIES LATER

A lady who managed an early post-war amenity that was a significant provision in the baby boom within the town, retired to Eastbourne. Miss F. W. Mosley moved to the new Oakhurst maternity unit in Anchorage Road in 1946, from a similar post at Bromley, after Mayor, Ald. F. W. Berry launched a highly successful financial appeal shortly following the war. Hundreds of mothers were grateful for the facilities provided in Sutton, with nearby public transport to all areas of the Borough, and into Birmingham and Walsall. The News commented, "Many people in Sutton are indebted to her."

DEMAND FOR NECESSARY RESOURCE

Two A.G.M.'s stressed the urgent need for a Sutton Coldfield located swimming bath, eliminating the inconvenient, time wasting and costly excursions to Erdington and other parts of the City. The Boldmere Swimming club and Wylde Green Scouts pressed the point at their independent meetings. There was considerable support from other recent and long established groups and many local inhabitants. The Headmistress of a Boldmere school argued for an indoor Swimming Baths at the annual dinner of the Sutton Coldfield Business and Professional Womens' club, held in the Boldmere Hotel.

REDDICAP HILL FATALITY

A verdict of "accidental death" was returned by a jury at a Sutton Coldfield inquest on a 13 year old Falcon Lodge boy on his way home from school at the Riland-Bedford, pushing his cycle alongside a 15 year old friend, when he was hit by a lorry or van driven by a 30 year old pipe-layer of Walsall. The driver had lost his way going from Erdington – Coventry.

The 15 year old said both cycles had dynamo powered lights as they pushed the bikes, his on the pavement his friend in the gutter. A vehicle turned down the footpath brushing the hedge. About a yard from the younger boy's cycle the vehicle was moved back onto the road. The older lad thought the lorry's speed "was too fast for the hill it was on."

An independent witness at a subsequent magistrates court hearing told the bench, "he saw the van mount the pavement and travel along for 2 or 3 yards. While the vehicle was on the path he heard a bump, and afterwards saw the boy lying on the road." The driver pleaded not guilty, and denied mounting the pavement. He said, "it was drizzling at the time and the roads were greasy." The van driver was disqualified for 12 months, fined £15.00, and pay £2.13s costs.

The chairman of the bench told the driver "you have had a nasty jolt. We are just as sorry for you as you are for yourself, but on the other hand the public must be protected. It might have been worse with all the children coming out of school at that time."

Eleven new street lamps were later erected "at Reddicap Hill, at a cost of £405," the Sutton news reported. The Army authorities refused my application to attend the funeral of my, thirteen year old cousin, Peter Walker. "He was not a close enough relative," in the Army's opinion.

LONG TERM WATER PROBLEM

Sutton council noted with satisfaction, the Midland 'Red' agreeing to contribute 75% of the cost to divert the sewer in Holland Road to alleviate pollution of the Ebrook. It had been a long-term problem resolved.

FULL HOUSE IN SOUTH PARADE

Large audiences were recorded on each of the performances of the topical 'Holly and the Ivy', at Sutton's new theatre in South parade. There was excellent teamwork throughout the productions on the stage and behind. Freres considered, "The finished theatre will vie with any in the country."

BANANAS FOR EVERYONE

Lovers of fruit were delighted that there were sufficient bananas for everyone at Christmas 1953, widening potential variations in diets.

Looking back over their 1952/53 season, the Sutton Town under 16 football team remembered their Rotary Cup Final with pride. (Angela Hendley)

Reports abounded of definite improvement in the quality of toys with a comprehensive range, showing little variation to 1952 prices.

In common with most other parts of the country, Sutton Coldfield postal staff dealt with a record mail during Christmas 1953.

Our extended Christmas was not the same without peter, though I was pleased to be at home from the constraints of National Service for a short while.

For the 1953 Top of the Pops, John Platt of B.B.C. Radio W.M., selected; 'O Mein Papa'; 'I'm Walking Behind You'; 'I Believe'; and 'Rags to Riches.'

LICENSED TO WORRY

There may have been a cloud over thirty homes over Christmas with the knowledge, since Post Office Inquiry Officers had called in November, they faced prosecution over not having a radio or television licence; three days after Christmas.

The Sutton Coldfield Magistrates fined the 30 a total of £385.10.0d for not having set licences, twenty eight without sound licences and two having no T.V. licence. The two T.V. cases had television and sound sets installed and in working order. Some reasons given by defendants included: "I have recently had new furniture, for which I pay 21s a week"; "I thought a licence ran from January to January," and "I thought until I paid off my hire-purchase fees I would not require a licence." The defendants resided in 5 roads.

Chapter Four

1954 – SUTTON PARK – WORLD CHOICE

PROPERTY MARKET – NARROWING GAP
Estate Agents, H. Donald Dixon, reporting on the property market over 1953 commented on the "extreme scarcity of land in residential districts in and around Birmingham." Therefore, the company predicted it was quite likely that prices would "continue to harden." They also predicted the "very narrow gap between the cost of a second-hand house and those of a new house would continue to get smaller." Some new house buyers were realising that, by the time they had bought the plot, paid the architect and the builder, and laid out the garden, "the total cost is little short of the price of a good second-hand property."

Coronation Recalled. A historic picture 'Sutton Belle' (with 'Sutton Flyer' behind) pulls its first train since 1962 – the repaint was only completed the day before – waiting to leave Cleethorpes Lakeside station on the evening of 30th May 2003. (John G. Tidmarsh)

WALSALL TROLLEY BUSES IN SUTTON?

Suttonians, Streetly and Aldridge residents favouring the extension of Walsall Corporation Trolley Buses, from the Walsall boundary into the centre of Sutton Coldfield, seemed to be in the minority. The Sutton News reported a unanimous Council vote to oppose the Walsall Corporation's Parliamentary Bill, part of which "seeks to extend that town's transport system on further routes." It was recommended in a Town council meeting to oppose nine clauses of Walsall's Parliamentary Bill.

The chairman of Sutton's General Purpose Committee hoped that, when the proposed petition was lodged, it might be "possible to come to some agreement with Walsall Corporation." The Sutton spokesman, however, emphasised "Sutton Coldfield Corporation must protect themselves."

The clash of proposals by Sutton and Walsall brings to mind the Sutton Council's 1931 concern about the larger town's plan to introduce double deck buses through Streetly, Little Aston, Four Oaks and Sutton Coldfield. There had been concern for many years that the Midland 'Red' and Walsall Corporation bus passengers would take advantage of their elevated seating to observe rooms on the first floor and above on their routes within the Royal Town.[1]

NEW ESTATE SCHOOL

Relief was expressed on the Falcon Lodge with the opening of the new Junior School which had cost almost £50,000 to build. The News reported that "first year pupils had already been accommodated in two classrooms" and it was anticipated that second year scholars living in the area would be transferred from Victoria Road Boys' and the Town primary schools.

The Falcon Lodge Estate Residents Association's request for a Post Office on the estate was turned down. The current facilities at Whitehouse Common and Reddicap Heath were considered adequate for the time being.

C.B.E. AWARD

The importance of an encouraging and positive thinking teacher became a reality to me in my later years at the Victoria Road Boys' School as our Geography teacher, John Fishwick, shared his enthusiasm and knowledge with the classes that he taught. With his help, I gained encouraging marks and was pleased to learn later from the Sutton News that a man with the same name had moved from a special responsibility post at Boldmere Junior to become Headteacher at Minworth School.

---

1. Page 31 'Wheels Around Sutton', Brewin Books, 1997.

Another man, highlighted in the local paper in January 1954, was Alderman A.G.B. Owen of The Highways, Newhall Drive, who was awarded the C.B.E. for his work over 21 years in the Industrial Savings Movement. He was chairman of the West Midlands Industrial Advisory Committee and was sometimes referred to as the 'millionaire chauffeur'.[2]

SUTTON NEEDS A CREMATORIUM
With the growth of the Borough population and, in consequence, more deaths, the limited acreage for burials and the increasing popularity of cremation, the Sutton Coldfield Council decided to inform the Ministry of Housing and Local Government that Sutton Council "desired to be placed on the Ministry's list for a crematorium or crematoria."

SUTTON PARK AVAILABLE FOR JAMBOREE
The Chief Scout advised the local authority and the Chamber of Trade that "Sutton Park is in the district which is being considered for the Jamboree." The selected locality would be "accommodating something like 20,000 scouts from all over the world. The Park had great advantages." The Town Council endorsed a committee decision to invite the Scout Movement to hold its World Jamboree in Sutton Park during the summer of 1957.

T.V. CHANGING HABITS
The annual Licensing Sessions heard that the, 1949 built, B.B.C. T.V. Transmitter was projected to revolutionise family life with the introduction of television into Midlands homes. A solicitor was of the opinion that "a great many people have preferred to have their drinks at home, by their own fireside" since television came to Sutton Coldfield. This had resulted in these drinkers not going out to the public houses during the evening. A substantial number, however, had remained loyal to the hostelries!

NEW CHURCH OPENED
Falcon Lodge Hall was packed at the inaugural service on 6th February. The Reddicap Heath Road building cost £1,500 which was raised by a local Christian group working from its sister church in Duke Street in the town centre. The Sutton News described it as "the first church building on the Falcon Lodge Housing Estate."

Service leader, Mr. F. J. Wilday, "hoped that the people on the estate would regard the Hall as a spiritual centre and home." Mr. W. Day, an elder of the Duke

---

2. *P91/92 'Sutton Coldfield in the Forties', Brewin Books, 2003.*

Street Hall Open Brethren group, shared with the congregation that Alderman A.G.B. Owen had assisted in surmounting many of the difficulties – including obtaining the site and funding. Much of the work in furnishing and painting had been carried out by Christians from the Falcon Lodge and Duke Street fellowships.

The initial outreach work of Duke Street had included bussing children from Falcon Lodge to Sutton on Sunday afternoons, but the new Falcon Lodge Hall also provided mid-week activities for girls, boys and ladies.

Three of the Falcon Lodge Hall leadership team. Former Salvation Army officer, Harold Groves, a Chamberlains Manager, is on the left. In the centre is Church Secretary, Mr. F. J. Wilday and Mr. Peter Lyndon of Reddicap Heath Road. (Sutton Coldfield News)

LUNG CANCER: CONFLICTING REPORTS

In response to allegations that smoking had a detrimental effect on smokers' health, the Industry's research established that there was no proof that smoking caused lung cancer. However, an item noted in 'Millennium – The Century, Day by Day'[3], also recorded an independent study on the same subject which found that lung cancer was linked to smoking.

The Public at that time was thus presented with conflicting evidence about the connection between smoking and lung cancer. Smokers and potential smokers had to make up their own minds.

TEN MILLION LISTENERS

The same publication, 'Millennium – The Century, Day by Day'[4], also pointed out that in mid-February the 800th episode of the BBC Radio's 'The Archers' had a record audience of ten million.

ABOVE NATIONAL AVERAGE

Sutton parents learnt in the News that 11-17 year olds in the Borough had an almost 50% better chance of a Grammar School place than other locations.

---

3. *P775 'The Century, Day by Day' D.K. 1999.*
4. *P754 'The Century, Day by Day' D.K. 1999.*

Miss M. Rothwell, Headmistress of Sutton Coldfield High School for Girls, found "very few children who ought to have a grammar school education are missing out." The Headmistress believed that "35% of the 11-17 age group" have a grammar school education in the local area. From her information "the rest of the country is about 19%".

ANGLICAN AND METHODIST ACTIVITY

A Falcon Lodge resident made Sutton Coldfield News readers aware that the area was part of the Anglican Parish of Holy Trinity, Sutton Coldfield, and the new church, St. Chad's, built on Hollyfield Road in 1929 was a daughter church of Holy Trinity. The writer pointed out that "the whole of the Falcon Lodge Estate lies within a one mile radius of one of the most beautiful modern churches in the Midlands."

According to the same writer, many residents of the estate and their children attended St. Chad's Church's services and activities. The St. Chad's Church member clarified that the adults and children "had done so since the estate first opened and long before Duke Street began activities locally."

It was not clear whether Falcon Lodge children were bussed to St. Chad's, but they certainly were to the South Parade Methodist Church and the Wesleyan Hall. The average attendance of Sunday School scholars in 1953 was "179, plus the children coming by special bus from the Falcon Lodge Estate" according to the Sunday School Superintendent. He also said that he and the teachers hoped to contact as many homes as possible on the Estate during the Spring of 1954. The Youth Fellowship in South Parade "now had 100 members and could not accept any more for the time being."

Wesley Groves provides another view of the Falcon Lodge Hall beginnings. "Frank and Rita Wilday led a team from Duke Street in setting up a new church on Reddicap Heath Road." Wesley's parents, Harold and Doreen Groves, who had previous experience as serving officers in the Salvation Army, "were invited to share the leadership of the new church from the outset." Some further families involved in the new church were the Lyndons, the Barwells, Alan Dixon and Fred and Vera Smith.

Wesley described the 1954 building as having a brick frontage behind which was an ex-army prefabricated wooden hut which served as the main church hall. Through the 1950s the wooden hut was crammed with adults and children every Sunday and most evenings through the week. The church grew quickly in the 1950s through many child and teenager activities.

CENTRAL SUTTON FAMINE

At the annual Chamber of Trade dinner in the Town Hall, the guests heard that, similar to many other towns, "Sutton was suffering from the prevalent disease known as 'car park famine'!" This was due to the increasing number of vehicles on the roads. The President of Chamber warned "The parking problem was serious today, but it is likely to prove still more difficult when the streets and roads become more congested due to increasing traffic."

GREEN METAL HALL

Richard Shrive "attended St. Chad's Church in Hollyfield Road, where the vicar was Rev. David Loake, a very caring and quiet pleasant man." Mr. Shrive was confirmed in the C. of E. by the Bishop of Aston, at St. Chad's. "Richard was a member of the St. Chad's Scouts who used to meet in a green metal hall in Whitehouse Common Road." The scouts used "Rectory Park for games and tracking."

SUTTON AND ERDINGTON COMBINED CONSTITUENCY

Sutton Council lodged an objection with the Boundary Commission over the proposal to combine the Borough with the Erdington ward of Birmingham to form a new Parliamentary Constituency. The Chair told council members that politics must not enter into this matter. "We should be concerned only with the preservation and independence of this Royal Town."

Birmingham City Council, the News told its readers, debated the issue for nearly two hours before the City commended a committee's action, by 76 votes to 52, to support the Boundary Commission's plan. However, Birmingham urged the Socialist amendment, "that Sutton should retain its identity", to be implemented.

SPORTING MOMENTS

About the time of the year when Roger Banister had broken the four-minute mile barrier at Oxford during a match between the University and the Amateur Athletic Association, James Hogan, an international football coach, spoke about football styles at the Parkfield Amateur Football Club annual dinner. He claimed that football style in the country had deteriorated with the use of the 'big boot', aimless kicking the ball up in the air, and a 'go-in-and-get-it' attitude. The game had been spoilt. Mr. Hogan, a coach with Aston Villa F.C., felt that the English game had lost its prestige in international football. The coach proposed that the English style should get back to the 'three Rs' of football: brains; ball control and body balance. With the 'three Rs' constructive intelligent moves would be seen again in the national game.

Holland Road based Sutton Stars cycle speedway team won their first home fixture 53½-38½ points against Lambeth Aces. Dave Hemus was the top scorer with 11 points. The Farthing Lane brothers, Colin and Bryan Stonehouse, scored seven and five points respectively. Other Star riders were Hawkins, Bond, Slater, Tuffley and Bott. Local teenagers enthusiastically encouraged the Sutton team and the cyclists really became stars as they raced around the small compact circuit by the side of the Ebrook.

NOT ON A SUNDAY

In an attempt to boost attendance at the Shelsley Walsh Hill Climb competition, the organisers moved the event from a Saturday to a Sunday. Alderman A.G.B.Owen, the owner of the B.R.M. organisation, said this conflicted "on religious grounds with his principles" and withdrew his company's vehicle from the competition. The News reported that the B.R.M. Headquarters' staff tried to get Alderman Owen to change his mind and the Hill Climb champion, Ken Wharton, even drove the car in the Saturday practice. The Alderman's point of view may have had echoes of Eric Liddell's similar stand in the later film 'Chariots of Fire'.

PETER USTINOV'S PRIZE

A Sutton theatre company was cock-a-hoop at winning a nationwide competition organised by the British Drama League. The competition encouraged amateur groups to present new plays and the Highbury Little Theatre Group was one of twenty that took part. Mr. Adrian Stanley, playwright and producer, saw all the performances including Highbury's 'Love and Lunacy in March', which was written by Peter Philips.

The Premier award, the Peter Ustinov Prize, was received by Mrs. Lilian Fletcher, the Sutton producer, at the Scala Theatre where the finals of the British Drama League's annual Community Drama Festival was held.

INDEPENDENT GAIN

A letter by 'Carsher' in the June post-bag of the News stated that "The reason why Sir. John Mellor has now taken his stand as an independent seems to be of little consequence." To 'Carsher', what mattered was that "Sir. John had now left the degrading atmosphere of party politics. He must feel considerably refreshed."

FOOD RATIONING ABOLISHED

Some local Sutton Coldfield butchers gave their forecasts about the situation after food rationing was to be abolished. Mr. J. Allsop said "I don't think people will have any more to spend than they are spending now." Mr. Allsop was chairman of the Sutton Buying Committee which was to be disbanded.

Mr. M. C. Simons, the manager of Smarts the pork butchers, considered that it would be a difficult first six months for customers and the butcher and he anticipated that the wholesalers would raise prices. Butchers, according to Mr. Simons, were working on a much finer profit margin and "it is far less now than it has been for years" he told a reporter.

The Lamb Shop manager, Mr. T.C. Emery, thought the "best cuts would be slightly dearer for the first week, but the housewife will spend according to her pocket."

Mr. G. A. Lawrence, the manager of Marsh and Baxter, expected the "de-rationing will give the customers the benefit of service and civility." He closed his forecast with "they were sure to go where they are well treated."

According to the 'Millennium - The Century, Day by Day' on P761 "Housewives ceremonially tore up their ration books in Trafalgar Square at the end of all rationing after 14 years." The National Federation of Housewives promised to patrol all butchers with their notebooks to check on prices. Subsequently, Chamberlains (Wishaw) brought down from the North a herd of Aberdeen Angus Pedigree cattle to be specially reared on the firm's farm at Wishaw. Each week as "the beasts reach prime condition they will be slaughtered and sent direct to the Birmingham firm's shops." Mr. Arthur Chamberlain told the Sutton Coldfield News that "they had requested that a good proportion of the meat should be sold in Sutton Coldfield."

At the first Atherstone free fat stock market since 1940 no spectacular price increases were noticed. Clean cattle were averaging £7.8s.0d. per cut with a top price of £7.16s.0d. There were no signs of the so-called 'butchers rings'.

HOUSEWIVES' LEAGUE STANDS FIRM
Sutton Coldfield Housewives' League decided to boycott dear meat so that prices were bound to come down. "Butchers" the H. L. believed "cannot keep the meat for ever." They pointed to previous successful boycotts of eggs and vegetables which had forced prices down. "Our meat boycott would be successful", they promised.

ALTERNATIVE TO MEAT
Local people seeking an alternative meal from meat may have been pleased to learn that the Royal Vesey Fish and Chip saloon in Lower Queen Street had reopened under new management. The new owners advertised that the saloon was five minutes walk from the Odeon Cinema and open nightly until 11.15p.m. on Monday to Saturday. This enabled cinema goers to call in on their way home for a late take-away supper.

I recall that at Christmas time at least one other Sutton fish and chip shop gave children a free meal to take home.

The Farthing Lane shop produced a tasty fish and chip meal, but whilst I was at school, I became addicted to the 'Riland Road' menu and ate many a bag of chips over the years between the shop and my Jerome Road home. During W.W.II, Ted Flanagan pioneered a takeaway service from the same Riland Road premises.

JUVENILE DELINQUENCY DIMINISHING

Sutton Coldfield Ladies Circle heard that juvenile crime in the Birmingham area had dropped by 15% in the first part of 1954.

Mr. Hamilton Baynes, chairman of Birmingham Juvenile Court panel, reported that "indictable offences concerning juveniles had dropped from 1,518 to 1,229 in the year 1952-53. Delinquency was an inevitable product of the war and, now that children born during the war or immediately after were growing up, it was decreasing." He hoped that the figure will "return to a steady and more normal figure." No corresponding figures were given just for the Sutton Coldfield area.

NEW HOUSE PRICES

New freehold or leasehold detached houses were for sale in the Sutton area. There was a choice of four designs; all with three bedrooms and a garage, and the prices included fencing and road charges. In Blackberry Lane leasehold prices were £2,100 and freehold £2,450 whilst in Slade Road the prices were £2,150 and £2,500 respectively. With a 10% deposit, 90% mortgages were available.

TROW FAMILY SECRETS

'Sutton Coldfield in the Forties', includes a number of individuals' recollections of the delicious ice cream brought at Trow's Milk Bar on the Parade. There was a seating area at the rear which looked towards the Lichfield to Birmingham railway line and I, along with many other adults and children at the end of W.W.II, waited for my first taste of real ice-cream in a dish with a spoon.

In 1954 52-year-old Mr. Gregory Hainsworth Trow was interviewed in his parade café by the News. Apparently, his "grandmother pioneered the ice cream trade in the Midlands." With pride he told the reporter that "she was selling it in West Bromwich and she was using a recipe to produce soft, creamy ice cream long before I was born. There used to be hundreds of recipes before the war." Their ice cream was heat treated well before new health regulations made it compulsory. "Eating ice cream in the winter time is a recent development" continued Mr. Trow.

The Trow family "used to be glad, in those days, when the summer business was over" said Mr. Trow. "Making ice cream by hand was tiring work", he admitted. Mr. Trow came to Sutton Coldfield before W.W.I, "remembering the City Battalion and the ANSACS occupying the Park." Doreen Groves, one of the leaders of the new Falcon Lodge Hall, told son Wesley that "one of her favourite shops on the Parade was Trows." Mrs. Groves, however, was attracted to Trows "because of the Tea Shop" not the ice cream!

CLASSROOM DISTURBANCE

Alan Smith from Boldmere seemed to have a propensity to get himself into situations in school that led to corporal punishment. When talking about a teacher at senior school, he said "I can still smell the smoky breath from his fags and can picture him riding his clapped out bike to school." "Someone," he told me, "had brought into school some sections of a motor inner tube which had been flicked around the playground. Somehow or other the motor tyre rubber landed at the feet of the teacher!" Result: three strokes on the backside using a lump of wood.

SUTTON LINES' SEMI-FASTS

Whilst I worked at Four Oaks and Blake Street stations, and also during the two years that I was away, the morning semi-fast service was treated as the lines' express.

Driver Brian Clarke informed me that, in order to form the 8.00a.m. from Lichfield City, the train crew had to book on at Monument Lane engine shed about 5.00a.m., take the light engine to the carriage shed, move the non-corridor stock into New Street and be ready to leave at 6.22a.m. for all stations to Lichfield. Only three minutes was allowed for the guard and the platform staff to unload many fish boxes at Erdington! After the engine had run round the train at Lichfield, it left all stations to Wylde Green and then fast to New Street, missing out Duddeston where tickets were usually collected.

The carriage stock and engine left Monument Lane station at 5p.m. to become the 5.17p.m. ex-New Street return semi-fast service with first stop Wylde Green. (Compare that with the 21st Century sweating of assets!)

ONE YEAR NATIONAL SERVICE TO DO

Looking back on my first of two years National Service, my request to be considered for the Military Railway at Longmoor was translated into lorry driving instruction. This I eventually failed and was put on building Bailey bridges and digging holes – many of which were filled up two weeks later! Although I was based in Kent, with the use of railway 'quarter fares', it was possible to be in Sutton Coldfield most weekends, keeping up with developments and still worshipping at Duke Street Hall.

Apparently, being 'kind of religious' was known to some on the Royal Engineers' camp. One morning whilst digging a large hole with other sappers, the sergeant sent a corporal for me and told me to go and see him immediately. Having made myself as presentable as possible in my semi-dirty denims and muddy boots, he ordered me to go and see the sergeant major at the double. Walking as smartly as possible, saluting passing officers on the way, my mind was racing away

A fellow sapper at our Royal Engineers camp at Hoo, in Kent. He gave me a lift to the mile Oak, on the A5, as he made for the north west. The dreaded Office of the Sergeant Major was in the building on the right. (Author)

reminding me of recent errors that the S.M. had probably decided that it was time to confront me with. Similar to flashbacks at the close of a film, the worst errors returned for a second time to impress on me what the S.M. had in store for me.

Making sure that the beret was in the position over my right eye, just as I had been told on many parade ground inspections, I nervously knocked on his door. "Come in!" was the short, terse, authoritarian reply. Fortunately, I remembered to restrain from saluting as he had dealt with me previously about that matter – "You only salute Officers, man." (This had encouraged me, since other sappers who had riled him were often challenged about their sexuality!)

THE UNEXPECTED!

If the sergeant major had graciously given me paper and pen to write down my most grievous errors, I would not have been able to do it as my mind had gone blank.

The sitting, but still tall, upright and immaculately dressed figure of the S.M. looked directly in my eyes and barked "Is it true what I have heard about you, Bassett?"

Here was the crunch – my last major disgrace was to be exposed. Without waiting for the reply which was still being choreographed in my numbed mind, he continued, "I understand from other unit personnel that you possess a Bible on the camp." If you had to have permission to have a copy of the christian scriptures in the barracks, it was a new one on me! Could I be charged with possessing a Bible? It would never have been on my list of possible offences. Fortunately for me, a soldier was allowed to have a Bible on the camp and the intriguing reason for my presence before the sergeant major was revealed. Having established from my faulty, nervous response that his information was accurate, he asked a favour! It was certainly not an order, but, if I did not agree to the request, it would cause some embarrassment to the unit management team, including the S.M. I thought of all those extra duties that would be coming my way....

"Can the C.O. borrow your Bible for a court-martial tomorrow in the camp so that the defendant can swear on it? It appears that you have the only Bible on the camp." I quickly agreed and I never found out who the accused was, the charge, or the result. As far as I know, the favour did not get me any less or more attention from the S.M.

Some while later, I was offered and accepted a midweek Christian Leader course in Surrey even though I had not requested it.

Sitting among the tyres the young woman at the back, met Keith Graham at the depot, they later married. (Keith Graham)

FIFTH ANNUAL FLOWER SHOW

Sutton's Park Forester Mr. Tom Allen was a significant supporter of the Town's Flower Show, which was part of the annual Horticultural Show held on the Meadow Platt in Sutton Park. The 1954 Flower Show programme included Mr. Allen's Gardening Calendar with a check list for each of the twelve months. During the one and a half day programme there were dancing demonstrations by pupils of Burcot Grange High School, and a children's Gymkhana, organised by Major Fisher of the Park Road Riding School. The Sutton Coldfield British Legion Band gave four, half hour programmes on the Saturday and two obedience tests were given by the Alsatian Association. An interesting additional attraction was provided by Mr. F. J. Field a handwriting expert.

The prize money for first prizes ranged between £4 and 5 shilling, seven cups or shield and a number of medals awarded. Local advertiser's were; The Sutton Coldfield news; Tudor Rose Hairdressing, Lichfield Road; J. K. Bourne & Sons Ltd, the Parade; Wyndley Nurseries, Clifton road; J. P. Morgan & Co, South Parade and Boldmere Road; Wrights Stores & Bakers, corner of Station Street and Park Road; with a back cover promotion by L. W. Sims of Chester Road north. Mr. Allen found the overall programme very demanding as the Hon. Show Secretary, yet satisfying, to see the high standards reached within the Town, during the July show.

BLACKROOT TIMBER MILL

The summer activities of the Parks Department required additional seasonal staff with a permanent compliment of about 40. Tom recalled the Blackroot Timber Mill "was always a hive of activity. We had a circular and band saws for converting our homegrown timber." There was a tractor adapted for agricultural work and general use plus trailers etc. A selection of hand tools applicable for estate work were also kept.

BRADNEYS AND WILSONS

These are two particular shops that have childhood memories for David Whitehouse. Bradneys was a favourite Boldmere place that he visited. There in the sweet-shop he was able to buy aniseed balls, Refreshers and Wrigleys chewing gum. The second shop, on the corner of Boldmere and Jockey Road sold basic equipment that he used in Sutton Park. Wilsons, amongst other things, sold fishing nets that the young boy found could assist him in catching fish. He also "caught sticklebacks in the stream that crosses Wylde Green Road on its way to Penns Hall."

FRERES IDENTIFIED

Freres, the writer of regular columns in the Sutton News, had a real insight into Sutton life. Items on a diversity of subjects were noted in the Freres Centre page spread, a number being referred to in this series of local history books about Sutton Coldfield.

A Sutton News reporter in the mid-fifties, John Wood, wrote, "You ask about the 'Freres' column. 'Freres' was everyone and no one. It was the title of the gossip column for odds and ends. Items were contributed by all the reporting staff and, in my time, collated by the editor, Wilfred Clarke."

IMPOTENT ROAD SAFETY COMMITTEE

A local Alderman was of the opinion that the "shocking state of the roads and the flood of second-hand cars was making the 'Road safety Committee impotent to deal with accidents." To him the width of the roads "is my chief objection." They were not wide enough to take the tremendous amount of traffic being put on them. He also added the dangers of "narrow bridges and bends."

In the spokesman's view, "I believe you can get a second-hand motor car without any deposit." "That," he anticipated, "will mean an increase in the number of vehicles on these inadequate roads." He also suspected that many of the vehicles would not "be mechanically fit" to be on the streets.

CURATE'S PLEA

The Revd. David Loake, the curate in charge of the Falcon Lodge estate, was disappointed that there was no immediate sign of a meeting place for the St. Chad's and Falcon Lodge people who wanted an Anglican worship approach. Mr. Loake found that there was "no sign of a meeting place on the estate before 1955" and made a plea to the residents "to let us meet in your homes for religious meetings and classes."

BLABBS COTTAGES

Residents of Blabbs Cottages, Coleshill Road, were devastated when workmen "started clearing a way through their gardens", without any warning. Trees and hedges were later bulldozed down and a huge trench dug across the gardens.

Four days after the workmen had started, the cottage residents received notice to quit from the Church Commissioners' solicitor and "11 days before the notice came into force." The land at the rear of the cottages was to be developed for industrial purposes. The development had been "approved by Sutton Coldfield Corporation."

Some months later, one of the occupants "received substantial damages. The notice to quit was a mistake."

YE OLDE FOLKS' SPECIAL BUS

The Sutton Coldfield Old People's Welfare Committee's 'Ye Olde Folks' Special Bus' made its first appearance in August 1954, (P37-38, Wheels around Sutton, Lichfield and Tamworth, Brewin Books, 1997). It was an ex-London transport AEC 'Q' vehicle with a side engine. The bus was overhauled and adapted for old and handicapped people free by local firms – the seats being set "further apart than on a normal coach to give extra legroom for old and handicapped folk. A ramp could be lowered to give easy access for wheelchairs and beds." There were thirteen people on a trip to Kings Bromley – the oldest being 87 year old Mrs. Annie Marsh.

BEDFORD ROAD CYCLE CHAMP

A local cyclist certainly put his best foot forward to win the Liverpool-Edinburgh cycle race in 9 hours 16 minutes – beating the previous record by four minutes.

Bob Maitland's 210½ mile race began at 5.30a.m. and he was delayed by two punctures en route! (Bob was a Tour de France entrant and is still an official of the Concorde Cycling Club.)

ILL TREATED HUSKY DOG

A Husky dog was struck by a walking stick and a pickaxe by his owner, a Sutton labourer. Another dog was kept in his possession without a licence. The man was fined on both offences and ordered to cover the veterinary and witness costs. The "Husky recovered, but could not walk more than 100 yards without pausing for a rest," said a witness.

J. ARTHUR RANK INNOVATION

There was some fast footwork at the end of a July evening performance when the ordinary screen at the Odeon Cinema was replaced overnight by a curved screen. The Sutton installation was part of J. Arthur Rank re-equipping its cinemas to meet the new trends in the presentation of modern films.

FIRST IN THE COUNTRY?

Sutton's Institute of Further Education claimed that its Cookery Class for men maybe the first in the country. Led by Mrs. Barbara Tinley, the sixteen men represented many backgrounds which included chiropodist, dentist, electro-plater, journalist and librarian. Mrs. Tinley, a housewife, thought the "men would be less difficult to instruct than the housewives" in her other eight classes. The 16 were amongst 1,000 people who enrolled for the day and evening classes that began in September 1954.

SUTTON PARK WORLD JAMBOREE CHOICE

The 1870 founded Sutton News recorded a decision which may have been one of the most significant decisions that it had reported in 84 years of publishing. The front-page story reminded readers that the choice had been predicted by the News four months before in the issue of May 21st. The Park had been chosen by the Boy Scouts Association as the venue for the Special World Jamboree and Rover Meet to take place in August 1957.

It would be the largest Jamboree in the history of the Scout movement with 35,000 people from scouting centres all around the world. They would camp in 600 of the available 2,400 acres. Readers were informed that this special occasion would be held out of the usual four-year sequence to mark the Jubilee year and the centenary of the birth of the founder, the late Lord Baden Powell.

IMPOSSIBLE WITHOUT ENORMOUS DAMAGE

A committed scouter, who attended the last world Jamboree in this country at Birkenhead in 1929, warned that there would be damage to the beloved Park. As Chair of the Friends of the Park, he said that "the committee would be sorry to see the Park damaged." They balanced that factor against an event of such national importance that "it should not be opposed." Major. Fred Monk continued in the News interview, "Believe me, it is impossible to run a Jamboree without enormous damage, though none of it is malicious, of course." In part of this balancing act, Major. Monk reminded readers "On the other hand, the benefit to the Town will be enormous."

YOUTH SERVICE APATHY

A number of contributors, including those in 1951, praised the work of the Sutton Coldfield Youth service, but John Edgerton, Chairman of the Youth council, hoped "the Youth service plans for 1954-55 would bring them out of the apathy which had to be characteristic of the past year." The attendance at the Methodist Youth Club, however, appeared to be successful.

MARRIAGE BREAKDOWN

Modern marriages were "presenting more difficulties than in the days of our grandparents", Mr. G. Clark of the Marriage Guidance Council stated. In those days the M.G.C. advised, "The wife had no chance to argue!" Now, with the equality of the sexes, "a better type of marriage was possible." Mr. Clark found that the causes of modern divorces are usually "a lack of determination and sense of responsibility."

This rough R.A.F. 216 M.U. football team may have caused the R.A.F. Regiment members some headaches if they met on the football pitch. Corporal Keith Graham is on the extreme right of the front row. (Keith Graham)

R.A.F. – OCCASIONAL EXERCISE

An occasional exercise at the R.A.F. Station tested the Whitehouse Common personnel's state of training and war-preparations. This confined all to the camp. During the night, infiltration tactics were attempted by 'saboteurs'. Next day an air attack on the installation was carried out by ground forces of the R.A.F. Regiment. Thunder flashes and smoke candles were used to create realism and headaches for the defending airmen and women.

HEADACHE FOR FARMERS

In 1954 there was still a shortage of part-time helpers to harvest the potato crop and, as during the autumns of the late 1940s, schoolchildren were still released from their classes. This headache for local farmers was highlighted in the 'Warwickshire Farmer' the county organ of the National farmers Union. Mr. R.H. Robinson wrote that it was a very trying time "in the north of the county." The official was endeavouring to find between "250 and 300 hands for the potato harvest."

U.F.O. SIGHTINGS
For the second time in a year the News had reports of objects resembling 'flying saucers' seen in the skies north of Sutton. Two neighbours in Shenstone Ward End drew the objects that they had seen and their pictures looked like coat hangers.

ANGLO-GERMAN RELATIONS
Erdington Rotarians learnt from a member of The University of Birmingham's Extra-Mural staff that Britain was facing a "completely new relationship with Germany, a country with which she had been in two major conflicts this century." Nine years ago Britain talked of disarming Germany, now they "are talking of re-arming her."

"Germany", Miss A.M. Grutter, a recent Foreign Office visitor to Germany said, "had emerged as an equal partner once again in Western Europe." "In the last nine years", Miss Grutter informed the Rotarians, "two post-war Germanys have appeared with two Presidents, two Chancellors and two totally different political systems."

Answering a question from Mr. Elyde, the speaker recognised that "the French were naturally horrified with the idea that their traditional enemy was becoming strong again." As a nation, the Germans worked longer hours for relatively less money than people in this country. Miss Grutter added "They are extremely good soldiers and the Germans respond to exterior discipline without question."

"The Germans", pleaded the speaker, "had shown, since the war, every sign of being democratically minded." They said "the past should be forgotten." She concluded with the question "Was there any alternative to re-arming Germany in view of the menace from the East?"

On the same page of the above News report on the Rotarian meeting, there was a Regular Army advertisement, which showed a soldier sewing on his third stripe as a sergeant. National Servicemen started at £1.8.0d per week with a regular on £2.19.0d. Soldiers had generous leave and an allowance of free travel warrants.

SUTTON PARK IN NOVEMBER
During a Natural History ramble, the Sutton society's November event recorded a number of bird sightings. At Wyndley, on a chilly damp afternoon, more than 80 coots, four porchards, numerous mallards and two swan families were observed.

Powell's Pool provided an unmistakable heron in customary leisurely flight with its huge and outstretched legs. There were small parties of finches flying over and a flock of redwings were seen. On marshy land a snipe suddenly rose, almost under the feet of the party.

Longmoor was almost deserted except for several tufted duck and a few moorhens.

Coronation Ride. John Tidmash in the centre, had cycled all over Sutton Park. Here in 1954, he explains his freelance model of a Roller Coaster, to Mr. W. Chivers, Physics Master at K. E. G. S. Aston with 3 other pupils. (John G. Tidmarsh)

The West Midlands Bird Club advised me, from their 1954 records, that nightjars were noted in the breeding season. In July and August, a pair of black-necked grebe raised a single juvenile – being the only breeding recorded that year in the West Midlands.

MUNIFICENT GIFT
Lord Bennett of Edgbaston's gift to the Falcon Lodge residents of a Community Hall on the council approved site at the junction of Newdigate and Churchill Roads brought an enthusiastic response. The new resource would be used by both social and religious organisations. The Borough Surveyor, Mr. T. Porter, was working on plans which would be submitted to Lord Bennett.

THIRTY NINE YEARS LATER
Mr. Arthur Corbett, the Mayor's Secretary through two world wars, retired in 1954 after 39 years service to the Borough. When he began in 1915 there were 22,000

people in the town in 5,000 houses, whereas in 1954 the population had doubled to 49,000 with a trebling of houses to 16,000. The Secretary "had thoroughly enjoyed his duties", and expressed his appreciation to the Town Clerk and his colleagues in various departments.

GREEN GROCERY THEFT
Wesley Groves wrote about the appreciation of Chamberlain's customers when they spoke of his father's dealings with the public. However, six staff of the respected and jovial George Rose, wholesale and retail greengrocer, were fined a total of £110 by Sutton Magistrates. The staff had stolen fruit and vegetables from Mr. Rose and then sold the goods to other greengrocers. The defending solicitor had been instructed to say "this sort of offence is very prevalent throughout the whole greengrocery trade."

SITUATIONS VACANT
The following are from a selection of vacancies in and around Sutton Coldfield advertised in November 1954:

Laboratory technicians at Aston Technical College. Senior grade £460-£520.
Choirmaster at Walmley Parish Church. Good organ and responsive choir. £52p.a.
Butcher. Smart youth, able to ride bicycle and learn trade.
Fish salesman and Blockman. Good wages for right man, excellent prospects – Chamberlains, Boldmere Road.
Furnace Bricklayer. Required immediately, suitable man aged 55 or under.
Forge Lane, Minworth.
Lorry Driver. General haulage, chiefly livestock and agricultural produce, over 20 years of age. E.W.Watts, Bassett's Pole Garages, Sutton Coldfield.
Single girls 15-25years. Permanent and well-paid posts. Five-day week with training given. Manager, Sutton Laundry, Coleshill Road, Sutton Coldfield.
Young man with Military service completed for export department of Erdington Company. Some experience desirable. Valor Co. Ltd., Wood Lane, Bromford.

BRITAIN MOTOR MARKET LEADERS
A News item predicted that when industrial historians look back on the middle years of the 20th century, "the fantastic performance of the British Motor Industry in the export market will excite comment."

In January to September of 1954 Britain sold £259 million worth of motor vehicles, parts, accessories and equipment which was a £35 million increase on the same nine months in 1953. Britain maintained her substantial lead over all competitors. Britain's closest export rivals in 1954 were the United States with the third largest exporter of cars and commercial vehicles being West Germany.

GREATEST ENEMY
In a Sutton Coldfield News Leader, compliments were given to various organisations that exist to improve workers' conditions. However, in the Leader's opinion, nothing was being done about the greatest enemy of all – air pollution.

GARAGE OWNER MARRIES
A well-known garage owner in South Parade, Frank Arnold of Victoria Road, married Miss Dorothy Gloster of Victoria Road. After the wedding reception, the couple left by car for an undisclosed honeymoon destination. Arnold's Garage was a landmark in South Parade.

COLOSSAL NUMBERS
The Chairman of the Town's Planning Committee advised Suttonians that "a colossal number of private houses are being built in Sutton, mainly for Birmingham people. Sutton had become a dormitory town of the City." The Councillor said "By allowing Birmingham people to build their own homes in Sutton, the Town was doing its part as far as the City's overspill was concerned."

T.V. AFFECTS SCOUT ATTENDANCE
A local District Commissioner of Scouts encouraged scout leaders to make scouting programmes "so interesting that the boy will forgo T.V., pictures, visits to aunts and other excuses, all put forward for absenteeism." The T.V. fever was very much affecting scouts' commitment.

WATER SWIMMING CLUB BEATEN
73-year-old Wilfred Wrench of Whitehouse Common Road left the regular Sutton Coldfield Winter Swimming Club members in the cold! Whilst there was "still a nip" in the water, the septuagenarian took the plunge into Blackroot Pool before the other less hardy members took part in the annual Christmas morning race.

Mr. Wrench and the other Winter Club members could have improved their circulation after the icy swims if they had listened and danced to John Platt's 1954 Top of the Pops selections which were: 'Rock around the Clock', 'Secret Love', 'Cara Mia' and 'Wanted'.

As the Town entered the New Year and looked forward to Sutton Park being the focus of the World Jamboree in 32 months time, the Sutton Coldfield residents were not to know of the national tragedy to happen in 1955, so close to home.

Chapter Five

1955 – NATIONAL TRAGEDY

LESS MUNICIPAL HOUSE BUILDING

Bad weather and labour problems were put forward as contributing factors to less municipal housing built in 1954 than in 1938. The recent figure being 193. In comparison, 512 private houses were completed in the borough.

GAP IN PRIVATE HOUSING MARKET

A Gate Lane News postbag contributor claimed "it seems beyond the builders ingenuity to cater for the very large, though neglected, section of the public". The writer referred to "the childless couples, over 40, or those whose family is grown up and left the parental home". Instead of the 3 bedroom houses many occupied, they only needed: one large living room, decent kitchen, one nice bedroom, perhaps a box-room and bathroom.

The reader argued "surely for about £1,800 this type of property would be a practical proposition", releasing their 3 or 4 bedroom type houses for those with growing families. The writer confided, "I would sell this style of 3 bedroom house at £1,800".

NATION OF SPONGERS

A men's organisation warned its members of a public trend that would lead to individuals abdicating their personal responsibility to fend for themselves. Instead of developing people into finer citizens, there were attempts to provide everybody with everything they needed, with no effort on their part. Such actions, the membership were advised, would create a nation of spongers and slackers.

NO RADIO LICENCES

A total of six Sutton Coldfield people in Riland Grove, Holland Road, Eastern and Victoria Roads were fined between 20s-60s on having no radio licence. All admitted the offences.

NATIONAL TRAGEDY

The afternoon of Sunday 23rd January 1955 was a fine, quiet, winter scene in Sutton Coldfield. People were out walking in the Park, some near the restful Blackroot Pool,

113

only a month before a hive of activity with families and individuals claiming bunches of Sutton grown holly. Even more recently the scene of Christmas Day swimming.

The last customers had made their way home from the Station Hotel for a late lunch and the nearby Sutton Police station staff had a chance to get up to date with correspondence and general admin. Similar to myself in eight months time the late turn porter at the L.N.W.R station had securely locked up the station on Saturday night, with coal fires prepared for customers awaiting the next local train service at 6.15a.m. on Monday morning.

John Wood a Sutton Coldfield News reporter was at home appreciating a time of quiet before the Monday post at the newspaper office and people calling in with the latest news for that week's edition.

A.A. Patrolman Geoff Dixon was on his motorcycle and sidecar monitoring part of his regular beat on the A446 and A452, frequently acknowledging the organisation's members with a smart salute. It was a fine Sunday afternoon with a few pre-spring motorists out. The traffic was on the light side. Tomorrow would bring traffic jams in a few locations, but that Sunday generally was a pleasure to be on the reasonably free-flowing roads. However, he was aware that in an emergency, being a patrolman with a sidecar-radio as part of an A.A. Experiment, he was contactable quickly.

Up from the Station Street Congregational Church halls and past the police station was the Station Hotel on the right and across the road the locked doors onto the up platform. (Mike Lewis)

Aston shed engine driver Ted Higgs was at home. Shift work could be disruptive for wife Muriel and himself, though through the years they had adjusted to the inconvenient times he had to book on and come home at all hours of the day and night. Thankfully there was remaining time that Sunday to enjoy each others company, away from the footplate and changeable weather conditions.

The Congregational Church caretaker had cleared up from the morning service in the Park Road sanctuary and Station Street church halls having had a breather before the evening worship.

SUNDAY PEACE BELOW

George Overton and his family, that resided in the station house below the booking office and wooden hill leading from the Lichfield side platform to the booking hall, appreciated the quietness of Sundays without staff and trains around.

With the postwar vote that Sunday Cinema opening should remain at the Empress, Odeon and Pavilion, time was approaching for the late afternoon preparation to welcome patrons at the Parade venue.

My weekend leave was coming to a close when I went along for the Sunday afternoon young people's Bible study in Duke Street Hall. A few more hours then I would be catching the trains back to Kent.

Two friends anticipated going along to Four Oaks station footbridge to photograph afternoon diverted express services and perhaps chat with the duty signalman, if he came to the box door. They knew most of the signalling staff, from regular visits to the station.

BURTON CONDUCTOR DRIVERS

Retired engine driver Norman Fenn, informed me the Burton motive powershed code of 17B, covered two sites. At Moor Street was the Midland Division section with express passenger traffic covering the Midland Main Line: Derby, Sheffield and the North, Birmingham, Bristol via Tamworth; also Manchester via Matlock and London St. Pancras.

The London North Western Division, Horninglow shed at Hawkins Lane had staff rostered on a few short passenger trains, but mainly freightwork. They had no booked express passenger trains.

The Hawkins Lane men travelled via Lichfield City to Sutton Coldfield, Aston Junction to Birmingham and Lichfield City via Brownhills to Walsall. Further North Western turns included services from Lichfield Trent Valley along the West Coast Main Line then Stafford and Crewe and the North Staffs route to Tutbury, Uttoxeter, Stoke on Trent and to Crewe.

FETCHED OUT OF CHURCH

Burton Horninglow driver Mr.Harold Allen, known as 'Dick' Allen on the railway, similar to Birmingham New Street inspector George Overton, was pleased to be off duty on Sunday 23rd January. An extended family member of Mr. Allen told me "it appears he wasn't due to be driving on that day and was actually fetched out of a Church service to go into work". The relative remembered him as a "nice man, a real giant size". He and his wife Maisie "did have a son, who sadly died as a baby" To Harold "he loved his job and was very dedicated to it. He was a very proud railwayman".

AN UNFAMILIAR ROUTE

Gloucester driver J.T. Martin and his fireman J.T.A. Howell knew the Class A Midland Division line of 42 miles between Birmingham and Derby, with a maximum of 75 m.p.h. but were unfamiliar with the Western Division Class C secondary route, between Aston Junction and Wychnor Junction, via Sutton Coldfield. The Sutton diversionary line had a maximum permitted speed of up to 60 m.p.h in places. The route ran across hilly country in a 'switchback' fashion with ruling gradients of 1 in 100 and considerable curvature, particularly into and through Sutton Coldfield on the up line to Birmingham.

Advance notices and arrangements provided Driver Martin with a local conductor driver from Birmingham to Burton -on-Trent on the northward journey, with him resuming as driver from Burton, arriving at Derby at 1.03p.m.

A ROUGH RIDE

After an almost two hour rest the Gloucester pair took over the 30 minute late running 12.15p.m. cross-country York - Bristol express. As they relieved the Sheffield men on engine Class 5MT 4-6-0 No 45274, which was working home to Bristol, they were told the engine was "riding roughly with some knocking in the axle boxes."

Station staff at Derby reduced the late running to 13 minutes from that town, but permanent way work to Burton increased the late arrival to 20 minutes in the Brewing centre, where conductor driver H.E. Allen of Burton (Horninglow) Motive Power Depot joined the engine at the platform. Like Driver Martin the 17B driver, brought on specially to release the previously booked Horninglow man, a non-family contact, advised; had signed for the weekly 'notices'.

INQUIRY REPORT

Quite a number of quotes from the subsequent Inquiry report by Lieutenant-Colonel G.R.S. Wilson and the A.S.L.E.F. 'The Locomotive Journal' are included. The Inquiry Report is available in the Sutton Coldfield Local Reference Library.

Leaving Burton, the 225 yard long train with about 300 passengers departed at 3.37p.m., 15 minutes late. Driver Allen was seated and Driver Martin standing behind him on the footplate.

The Inquiry Report confirms the train driver should remain on the engine, even if the conductor driver is driving.

RELIEF STATION MASTER

The Horninglow conductor driver safely negotiated the Wychnor Junction movement, taking the express from the Midland Division Main Line onto the Western Division diversionary route, 23¼ miles to Birmingham New Street.

Relief Station Master Roger Shenton was in temporary charge in the Lichfield Trent valley Junction signal box. (Roger Shenton)

23 year old Relief Station Master Roger Shenton, located at Rugby Midland Station, knew the Lichfield Trent Valley Junction signal box system. He was aware the duty signalman liked a drink at the Trent Valley Hotel before Sunday lunch at home. Roger unofficially took over so Jim could get his pre-meal drink. He was made aware by the Brookhay signalman of the "imminent approach of the York - Bristol express."

Mr. Shenton requested "Lichfield City No 2 signalman to accept the express forward"

Having received permission Roger "closed the level crossing gates, using the large metal wheel just inside the box doorway, then locked the now closed gates". The relevant signals were raised, bringing the cross-country train into the high level station.

Roger informed me "A stop was always taken at the water column in order that the locomotive could fill the tender tank. No passenger stop was advertised here."

An inside view of Lichfield Trent Valley Junction signal box, including some L.N.W.R marked apparatus. The white levers indicated they are not operational. The link line to the west coast main line bears down an incline to the right. (Colin J. Marsden)

LAST VEHICLE FIGURES

Mr. Shenton continued "while waiting for the express to depart I observed Lichfield resident Arthur Attenborough, a Birmingham New Street Station travelling ticket collector walk off the platform end and climb into the guard's van and sit opposite the train guard". On reflection the Relief Station Master advised me "I could plainly see both men as the last vehicle was an L.M.S.R. Brake Third Corridor with end windows and side look-outs".

When the express was ready to leave the driver whistled and moved off at 3.58p.m. Mr. Shenton advised the Lichfield City No.2 signalman, accordingly returning the starter signal to danger and sending the 'train out of section' to Brookhay signal box.

From the special working notices a Burton direction diversion express should be shortly offered from Lichfield City No.2 signalman.

UNCOMFORTABLE TO STAND

When the 12.15p.m. York - Bristol express left Lichfield Trent Valley station, conductor driver Allen and Gloucester fireman Howell were on the footplate. Gloucester driver Martin had left the footplate at the Trent Valley high level station, taking a seat in an empty compartment of the leading coach, because he found it uncomfortable standing up on the rough riding engine. Apparently it was a good opportunity for him to rest. In driver Martin's opinion, the conductor driver did not require his presence on the engine.

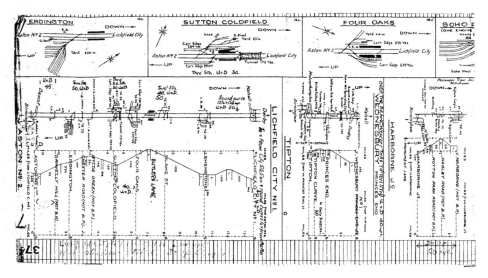

A gradient diagram of the railway route between Lichfield City No. 1 and Aston No 2 signal boxes with switchback effect. (L.M.R. [B.R.])

ON CAMERA

Railway enthusiast colleagues, Tony Reason and Malcolm Cooper realised their patience was being rewarded as they could hear a diverted express coming down the gradient from Blake Street towards the A38 over-road bridge. Tony excitedly waited for it to get closer to the Birmingham side platform and the footbridge. As the engine stormed under the footbridge, steam and smoke billowed around their vantage point.

Malcolm informed me that Tony said to him "this one is moving at a fair speed". With Mr. Reason's permission his action picture shows the train crews' determination to get to New Street as quickly as they could. Tony an engineering apprentice, thought the train was "running at about 45 mph and accelerating".

Signalman John Gilbert in the Four Oaks box "thought the engine was under steam when it passed his box" estimating the speed at no less than 40 mph. Schoolboy John Leake informed the Sutton Coldfield News "he had never seen a train going so fast past his house", which he commented about to his mother at their home at the side of the gradient towards Sutton tunnel.

"APPLY THE BRAKE"

Some years after the incident, the former Train Ticket Collector Arthur Attenborough shared with me, "I was travelling with the late Frank Harrison, the train's guard, to book on duty at Birmingham, then collect tickets on the

Mr. Reason's significant picture of the 12.15p.m. diverted train, two minutes before its tragic end. (Tony Reason)

Mr. Reason some years later, on the Llangollen Steam Railway. (Mrs. Reason).

same train from New Street". Arthur recalled "as the driver was coming over by the Bishop Vesey Fields, the guard and I thought the driver was approaching the tunnel too fast". Mr. Attenborough encouraged the guard to make a brake application. "The guard made a short three second brake application". Arthur heard the air intake into the brake valve as the brake was applied.

Arthur continued "at the rate the train went into the tunnel" he "did not envisage an accident but expected the train to lurch".

Mr. J.K. Langthorne and his girl friend were returning to Worcester from a visit in County Durham. As they came into Sutton tunnel "he took his girl friend into the isle of the carriage. They could tell it was coming off. They held each other, the carriage lent over to the right, with the wheels on the left hand side coming off. They slid from one end down the coach to the other end". It took them some time to get out.

Railway engineer Robert Paddison's view of the northern end of the Sutton Coldfield tunnel. (Robert Paddison)

A pre 1955 picture emphasises the curve into the station. The approximate point of the initial derailment is covered by the first vehicle behind 40633. Station Hotel chimneys are left of the nearest telegraph post. (Arthur Spencer)

"DID I HEAR SOMETHING?"

John Tidmarsh heard it happen. "We had just finished our Crusader Class in the old Conservative Rooms on the Parade (opposite the library)". Standing on the outside fire-escape at the back of the building he had an uninterrupted view across to the railway on the high embankment south of the station. The station was visible but not the tracks. He heard "the train coming through the tunnel, pausing for it to go past. It came out of the tunnel with a great roar. The locomotive's hooter was blown in two or three sharp blasts lasting a couple of seconds overall. As trainspotters we were focused 100% on listening and waiting to see the number. Then there was silence". He questioned if he had been mistaken, "but then a great column of steam rose from the station and I knew something bad had happened".

A.C. 2. Brian Graves joined the train at Sheffield Midland, Getting into the front compartment of the first coach. His mother, in the Sheffield newspaper sent to me by Mr. D.Wilshaw, said to her son, "I don't like the idea of that."- Brian being at the front of the train. According to the reporter "Just before the train reached the Sutton Coldfield station, one of his friends, another airman asked Brian to go back to the fifth coach and sit with him". As they reached the fifth coach the train began to rock. Mr. Graves escaped without injury when the coach overturned.

RUN TO THE BOX

Guard Harrison and Ticket Collector Attenborough were in the tenth coach at the rear of the train, which remained upright near the tunnel mouth and up platform ramps. The Warwickshire Police report recorded "the tenth coach remained on the line some 22 yards from the tunnel". When the train stopped Mr. Attenborough jumped out onto the ballast, running up the ramps. "There was a wheelbarrow" he told me, "although it was cold I took off my overcoat, jacket, scarf, cap and flung them on to the barrow. I batted up the platform. I didn't notice the things such as sleepers, sleeper chairs etc. littering the platform. I ran up to the signal box because I knew the Bristol - York was due. When they were on time they usually passed at Gravelly Hill".

An engine fireman travelling in the second coach had been thrown out onto the ballast through a gap in the coach.

EMERGENCY CONTACT

Although the closed box was switched out, the box door was unlocked and fireman Derek Smith, brushing aside his fortunate but traumatic escape from the second coach, reached the signal levers just before Mr. Attenborough. Derek was also aware a down side express must be near. Suffering from the trauma, Mr. Smith "was unable to speak on the telephone to control "the police report noted. Arthur simultaneously told "Smith the sequence of signals to push back so the northbound driver would be given the danger signals from the Wylde Green approach". At the same time the Four Oaks guard Billy Hart saw the York bound express crossing the Chester Road bridge.

Many people were involved in different actions at the same time. Mr. Attenborough rang an emergency sequence of bells alerting boxes of the crash. Passenger, Marine H. Swann, forced his way out of the locked Station Street doors, going to the police Station 50 yards from the station. The police staff on duty had heard the crash.

Supt. G.C. Gardner and Inspector F. Quinton had a quick look round. The Superintendent returned to the Police Station to summon assistance. Insp. Quinton remained at the station to organise rescue work etc.

Mr. and Mrs. N. Fairey, living on the Driffold, went onto the line to wave down the north bound express, but the train crew had already been warned by the efforts of Attenborough and Smith. The Driffold couple's action was appreciated by the railways and supporting services.

M.O.H. TO THE SCENE

Dr. Preston the Borough's Medical Officer of Health was washing his car, when he heard the crash. He reached the scene as soon as he could. John Dennis and his girl friend enjoying a walk in Sutton Park heard the crash, making their way to the scene, Mr. Dennis saw Dr. Preston caring for the injured on the crash site.

The severely damaged 45274, with steam escaping and chimney ripped off. (T. Reason collection)

UNUSUAL SOUND AT STATION HOUSE

The Overton family who lived in the old station house below the main Booking Hall, were sitting in the living room. Mr. George Overton told the Sutton News "we are used to the sound of passing trains, but this one made a very unusual noise" Mr. Overton continued "there was a roar and then silence, which you could cut with a knife". Daughter Marjorie rushed to the platform and then told her parents of the devastation. A number of the railway passengers were helped by the railway family that afternoon.

DOUBLE LOSS

18 year old Ian Andrews was a recent R.A.F. recruit, based at 216 M.U. Joining the late running service at Derby. His son Gary reflecting on his late father's journey on the 12.15p.m. express informed me "he said the train was going very fast and started juddering and shaking as he was looking out of the corridor window". His dad spoke of "two little girls were playing near him. I think they perished" he advised Gary. Mr. Andrews remembered "coming to, on his back with one leg crushed and trapped and the other ripped and torn in a 'bad way'". The pain took over and knocked him out. Ian was a keen cross-country runner, walker, climber and cyclist.

A.A. SERVICE

Mr Langthorne and his girl friend were able to climb out of the derailed wrecked train, down a ladder resting on the side of their carriage. Waiting to be of assistance was an A.A. Patrolman in his khaki uniform, including breeches and leather leggings. On the platform Mr. Langthorne saw injured passengers placed ready for ambulances to take them to hospital. The A.A. Informed me that their records showed a patrolman had attended the accident scene but the person was not named. (Fortunately a request in the Sutton Coldfield News in 2003 to find the A.A. Patrolman of 48 years before, brought a response from retired Mr. Dixon in ten hours!) Geoff "heard about the crash over the A.A. Radio on my motorcycle and arrived about 10 minutes later". He had no problem getting onto the station in uniform. Mr. Dixon had become used to traffic accidents involving cars.

A.A. Patrolman Geoff Dixon found the scale of the giant engine and mangled carriages "frightening". (Birmingham Post and Mail)

The scale of "such a giant engine and carriages mangled up was frightening" to him. He can still recall "the hissing of escaping steam and the smell, firecoals burning, shouting and general confusion. Helpers were already climbing over the carriages of the train, which was on its side, to assist and passengers were already emerging". There was a sense of frustration the rescuers experienced, without heavy lifting equipment. With the relief of people surviving the crash, "everyone knew there were others trapped inside".

Mr. Langthorpe and his girl friend were amongst a number the A.A. Patrolman helped. When the professional people with the back up and operational skills became available, he found a hurricane lamp and "went to the front of the train, wondering what had happened to the driver. It was at this time someone took a photograph, which subsequently appeared on the front of a national paper the next day". Later Mr. Dixon's A.A. Inspector joined him. Eventually the Inspector "decided that we had helped as much as we could".

NEWS REPORTER ALERTED

News reporter John Wood at tea time had a phone call at home from a friend telling him "he had just seen 'five ambulances' racing down the Parade". His friend did not know what had happened. John was about to phone the police when a second call, this time from a reporter colleague, who had been returning home from a walk in the Park. Approaching Manor Road railway bridge, he stopped in response to a man shouting from a train window of a carriage stationary on the bridge above. John wrote "the man explained that his train was unable to continue the journey because the line was blocked by a wrecked train in Sutton station". The passenger threw down a screw of paper containing change and "his telephone number and asked my reporter friend to telephone his home".

"COME TO GRIEF"

Having been made aware by Arthur Attenborough's bell code and control's instructions, following the Sutton accident, the Four Oaks signalman opened the door shouting to Malcolm and Tony, "That last passenger has come to grief". The young men cycled down to Sutton station. They found the "main entrance door open". Walking down the wooden hill on to the Lichfield side platform, Malcolm recalled "Looking left only the last of ten coaches stood upright". The crash site was quiet, with lots of steam. "They could see part of the derailed 72 ton locomotive. They heard no cries for help". When the bells of the emergency vehicles "could be heard arriving, they left the scene to avoid impeding the rescue procedures". There were other observers about.

STRATEGIC ASSISTANCE

Signalman John Gilbert using his railway training and initiative, alerted two members of his family that made their own significant, though not recorded contributions of post accident actions.

John ran from the Four Oaks box to his parents home, one of the four terraced cottages across from the locked goods yard. He informed his father, Jack. H. Gilbert, the ganger in charge of the maintenance for the 3½ miles of double track through Four Oaks and into Sutton Coldfield station, of the crash situation. The inquiry report noted John's father had been the Sutton ganger for 22 years.

The other Gilbert family railway member, having tea with his parents, was Sutton Coldfield (L.N.W.R.) Signalman William. Ganger Gilbert immediately set off on foot, with the necessary equipment inspecting the up line into Sutton station. He checked the rails, points, lineside furniture and any items that may have featured in the crash. Brother William caught the next Midland 'Red' bus to take charge of his Sutton Coldfield box, in readiness for breakdown trains, communication needs and local railway data for visiting inspectorate.

Dr. Preston worked alongside other local doctors until 8a.m. on Monday morning, spending over 15 hours at the mishap scene. The M.O.H. told the News, "all the local doctors turned out in force and did wonderfully well. I think all the doctors who were not required in hospitals were on the scene. We had all the equipment we needed and ample help". He added, "The mobile surgical unit did a really wonderful job".

Ticket Collector Arthur Attenborough travelling on his way to work in the last coach of the derailed express, was one of the heroes of the day. (British Railways)

Once Sutton Coldfield signalman William Gilbert was aware of the crash at his home station, he caught the next Midland 'Red' bus from Four Oaks, going straight on duty for thirteen hours. The picture shows him at Four Oaks, towards the end of his career. (Author)

The first injured passengers arrived at Sutton Coldfield Hospital on the Birmingham Road between Farthing Lane and Duke Street "a few minutes after the disaster" the News stated. Warwickshire Police recorded the three local ambulances arrived from 4.19p.m. and casualties were at Sutton Hospital from 4.30p.m. The June 1955 Ministry of Transport and Civil Aviation Railway Accident Report gave slightly later arrival times of the emergency vehicles. There were four or five nurses on duty on the afternoon shift but on hearing of the disaster, off duty nurses and doctors hurried to the hospital. Clerks, X-Ray staff and domestic staff arrived to see if their help was needed.

Patients already in the hospital, well enough, moved from their beds, making room for injured and shaken passengers. Extra beds were put up to augment the hospital's normal complement of thirty beds. Miss H.M. Harrison, the Matron told the News, "This hospital became a sort of casualty clearing station. They kept coming. Corridors filled with stretchers, various offices were used by those needing dressings".

Reviewing the accident staffing Miss Harrison with pride said "my staff were wonderful and most of the off-duty staff turned up. We did not have to send out a call to them".

WRONG STATION

Not all call-out information was accurate. John Whitehouse an Erdington based ambulance driver, covered the local area and Tyburn, Shard End to the Sutton Coldfield boundary. Birmingham accepted calls outside their area in major incidents. He recalled, "in the early afternoon he and his attendant responded to a reported rail accident". The watch dutyman took calls, noting them on a carbon copy pad. The top copy went to the responding machine and the second copy retained at the ambulance depot for future reference. The verbal and written call was to Wylde Green railway station. "On arrival" John informed me "everything was normal". He had two choices, return to Erdington D.3. Depot and report a false alarm or "take a chance to Sutton station and check. Could be a false address".

On arrival at the 1862/84 L.N.W.R. Station, there were "just a few staff available. We requested help with a stretcher over tracks and on to the platform. The help was gladly given". There was an "eerie silence, with only a faint hissing of steam from the loco on it's side". Two people were trying to "extricate the driver and fireman from under the coal deposited on them from the tender". The ambulance driver and attendant entered the first carriage. "The relief driver was sitting in his seat in a state of shock, apparently uninjured". They decided to take the first two injured passengers, "a lady with injuries to wrist and arm and a man with a badly injured leg". Both taken to the ambulance with further help from,

The precarious angles of the carriages add to this sombre view of the location, where seventeen people eventually lost their lives.
(Kirkman Studios / Alan Kirkman collection)

believed to be, station staff, and onto the "Accident department of Birmingham General Hospital entrance in Whittall Street".

John and colleague returned to the station finding the entrance unapproachable due to the location "surrounded by fire appliances and ambulances". They returned to their Erdington base. Further data about rescue services input can be found in Warwickshire Police Superintendent J.C. Gardner's report of 31st January 1955 in Cross City Connections, Brewin Books, 1990 pp. 25 - 26. There are some minor discrepancies between Mr. Gardner's report and that of the Inquiry Report by Lt-Colonel G.R.S. Wilson.

QUICK AND EFFICIENT DIAGNOSES
The Group Superintendent Radiographer, Mr. Dennis Wilkinson, "was just about to settle down to a quiet Sunday afternoon", when he received a 'phone call from "Sutton Cottage X-ray staff member, Mrs. Connie Ware telling him, "that there had been a nasty accident at Sutton station and she felt sure Mr. Wilkinson would be needed". He found "the hospital car park full of ambulances and police cars".

Dennis was impressed by G.P. Dr. A.B. Hodson, by the way "he quickly and efficiently directed patients to the most appropriate of the Birmingham hospitals". Dr. Hodson knew how to "diagnose clinically and without the immediate use of X-ray". To Mr. Wilkinson's great surprise, he only had to X-ray one patient. Dennis pointed out "other G.P.'s quickly came and gave their assistance".

CONSTANT BOILED WATER
When Station Street resident Mrs. Beatrice Hare realised the train crash had happened, she rushed downstairs to tell her husband, Alfred. Friends staying with them at the time went with Mr. Hare, helping passengers getting out of the train. The Hare's used their sitting room to rest shaken passengers, providing cups of tea. During the long night they boiled water for the mobile surgical unit parked outside their home.

Mr. and Mrs. Bernard Litherland according to the Sutton Coldfield News, sat in their Station Hotel living room when they heard the crash. One of the hotel's entrances is 15 yards from the Station Street doors to the booking office and Birmingham side platform. The Hotel licensees felt the living room furniture shake after the train "had roared into the station". Then there was silence.

Bernard immediately opened the Pub, with Mrs. Litherland making tea and coffee for the train passengers, serving 60 or 70 people. Injured people were taken into the kitchen, where Police Woman Joyce Cheshire attended to their injuries. "She did a wonderful job", the hostess commented to the News.

Similar to Station Street neighbours Mr. and Mrs. Hare, the Station Hotel hosts supplied hot water to the W.V.S. and "refreshments through the night for press reporters from all over the country".

Ray Showell and his wife can recall, "hearing the noise of impact", in their Station Road home "without knowing what it was".

A RAILWAYMAN'S REGRET
Railwayman John Tidmarsh was soon on the crash scene, heard from the back of the Old Conservative Rooms. John saw the engine, almost upside down with its wheels in the air and "I remember seeing the chimney, which had been ripped off, lying beyond the end of the Birmingham-bound platform, some hundred feet ahead of the engine. As Mr. Tidmarsh "walked round the engine he wondered if the driver and fireman were still in the cab which was completely blocked by debris".

UNREPORTED AURAL EVIDENCE
From the subsequent inquiry, the accounts that John read, "it was never established if the driver was asleep or incapacitated". Mr. Tidmarsh believes Driver Allen was awake "because he," John recalled, "as the train left the tunnel and entered the

station, I remember very clearly that the Stanier 'hooter' was being blown, not continuously, but two or three blasts. I am completely certain about this". The 'hooter' blasts were over in a few seconds. On reflection he "regretted that he did not go forward with this aural evidence" meaning that someone on the "footplate knew they were in trouble".

John thinks none of the Inquiry witnesses reported the hooter being blown. Mr. Tidmarsh's statement could have introduced further questions during the Inquiry, though the Police Station staff, the Overton family and Hotel couple did not mention hearing the locomotive's hooter.

MAJOR EFFORTS

Both the Railway Inspectorate and Warwickshire Police reports plus the Sutton Coldfield News, praised the superhuman efforts of all the agencies, clergy and local folk that worked together for the rescue and subsequent care of the injured and distressed passengers and the dignity shown to those who perished in the national tragedy.

NEAR, YET SO FAR

Walking down the Parade after the fellowship at Duke street Hall at 4.30p.m., I was intrigued to see ambulances at regular intervals with alarms blazing travelling towards the local hospital or to major Birmingham hospitals. Another pedestrian in an authoritative tone made me aware of the train crash that had happened very recently. Joining the crowds behind the railings at the open end of the Birmingham platform, not far from the signal box, the partly demolished roof on the Lichfield side was visible and stacked-up passenger coaches, with broken glass and rescuers around. The locomotive was a sorrowful sight, presumably having reached the end of its working life. There was some almost hushed talking, but the general atmosphere less than 20 minutes after the accident occurred was disbelief in our town. The observers were so near to the scene, yet so far away, from the critical area where life and death rescues went on as circumstances allowed.

IAN'S TRUE CONDITION

Ian Andrew was in a coma for a short time and rushed to Birmingham in a very critical condition. "He had spent some time in a hospital in Birmingham" his son Gary wrote and told me. In the City, his father "had various and numerous operations on his legs, hand, body and head. He had 150 stitches in his head alone". His earlier fears about the condition of his legs was more serious than anticipated. The young R.A.F. man knew "one leg was in a bad way and was sure to be lost". When he did awake he learned that "he had lost both legs between the knee and thigh, plus a little finger on his left hand".

PAT COLLINS LIGHTING

Community participation was in further evidence when powerful lamps from Pat Collins fair ground were rushed to the crash site. To assist in lighting the scene. Messrs W. Hastilow and F. Cannings of the Town's Public Lighting Department rigged 6 flood lights on the roof of one of the battered station buildings. Having completed that task, the two local workman worked with the M.E.B. and railway electricians to fix their lamps.

Perhaps including eighteen year old Ian Andrews, Mr. Hastilow shared with the News, "In my opinion the number who died would have been much greater had it not been for the wonderful way in which police and ambulance officers and others worked".

Each December from 1955, an inscribed Bible presented to the 1st Sutton Coldfield Sea Scouts by Mrs. Keith Thompson of Doncaster, is paraded into the Church. The inscription recorded Mrs. Thompson's appreciation for the troop's help to her at the accident. (Author)

SCOUTS TO THE RESCUE

Alan Smith said "a gang of older scouts and leaders were working on the roof of the scout headquarters in the Park and on hearing the smash went to the aid of passengers for a short while before all civilians were asked to leave".

One lady the scouts rescued later presented the scouts with an inscribed Bible. Alan added "Which to this day is paraded annually into the church, usually on the first Sunday in December".

R.A.F. INPUT

The Sutton R.A.F. 216 M.U. Camp that Sunday 23rd January 1955, had a limited number of personnel around, being duty people and those living long distances away, that weekend passes were not adequate enough for sufficient time at home.

Corporal Keith Graham, that weekend, was on duty Fire Picket at 216. He heard "A Tannoy call to all areas requesting all available personnel to report to give assistance at the train crash site". Around 13 were transported in a canvas topped wagon. Corporal Graham still remembers on arrival there was "destruction, confusion with hurried behaviour, fear and worry which all contributed to a scene of horror". Seeing the engine it "seemed to have dug into the platform" with the leading carriages in an awful condition "one sliding up over another at approximately 30 degrees". Against a background of "Steam or smoke there were distraught passengers everywhere. It was a shattering experience for a young person coming into contact "with a first witness of death". Subsequent rail incidents bring the 1955 memories back to him.

TEMPORARY MORGUES

Keith received instructions from Public Service Workers. "He collected unclaimed belongings taking them to the Station Street Police Station". Much of the possessions were "mostly in an awful condition". He also kept away "inconsiderate photographers taking pictures". The most traumatic exercise was keeping the access free to the waiting room on the up platform "which was being used for bodies". There remained an uneasy feeling in that room, eight months later when I cleaned it as the duty porter. The Corporal also maintained access for ambulance people treating some very seriously injured passengers. "The R.A.F. Support lasted for many long hours. The 216 M.U. personnel later received a 72 hour long weekend pass for their efforts that weekend".

Additional accommodation for the bodies was augmented by Mr. Ken Woodcock, the Highways Department Superintendent. His wife recalled he was able to provide temporary facilities in the "Riland Road Mess rooms, where the deceased were laid on tables". The Coroner's assistant prepared the "bodies for identification and visits" by parents, partners etc. Mr. Woodcock was "very distressed by the events".

Walter Roberts, a Sutton Coldfield lengthman thinking back to the incident, "we did what ever we could to help. The engine dome burnt itself out on the flower bed". He was astounded with the effect of the track under the locomotive and train. Mr. Roberts related "the rails were twisted up like wire".

Park Road resident, Mrs. Laura Cook, like many householders near the accident location, went to offer practical help. She told me "we did not hear the crash", but when they knew about it "my friend and I went up to see if they needed blankets or anything else". It was a very sad place for days, but police and first aid people were very good. "The Station Pub was used as a First Aid Post", Laura recalled.

STATION STREET REST ROOM

The Congregational Church caretaker, Mr. H.S. Grainger, was preparing for the evening services. His wife having heard the crash told him about it. He "ran into Station Street, finding it was full of ambulances". At the Police Station he found they were trying to get the names of passengers, giving them tea. The News observed "the passengers were in cramped conditions". The Police were grateful to accept use of the Congregational Hall. Mr and Mrs. Grainger made tea for about

120 people. The caretaker related the community spirit was shown, when folk realised the Grainger's stocks of milk, sugar and tea were running out, they went to their homes to bring fresh supplies. The News noted everyone "had gone by 6.30p.m.". When the Graingers "went to the station to help".

Mrs. Janice Moore, a local history researcher found evidence of a letter in 1955 from the Chief Constable of Warwickshire thanking the Park Road Congregational Church for the help "given in connection with the recent train disaster".

CINEMA TELEGRAM SERVICE
The Empress management had more people through their doors that Sunday evening than they had anticipated. The Sutton News recorded that quite a number of passengers on the ill-fated 12.15p.m. diverted express drifted from the railway station trying to find help, which they had not found elsewhere. On reflection, with 300 on the train and emphasis on the severely injured and dead, many would have had to seek out assistance on their own, when the town was normally quiet on a winter evening. Cinema manager Mr. J. N. Longley had passengers asking if they could have free telephone calls to relatives. "Many had lost all their money, wearing torn and blood covered clothing". Until quite late that evening his desk was littered with hastily written telegrams of reassurance for all parts of the country. Many simply said: "Rail accident. I am unhurt".

MOTORISTS ON CALL
While the Sutton Hospital catering staff prepared tea and sandwiches "throughout Sunday night", the Matron, Miss Harrison and staff had offers from Sutton Motorists to ferry stranded passengers. Some were taken as far as Stourbridge and Bridgnorth.

"Dozens of people", Matron advised the News "had offered to give blood", to provide supplies in case of transfusions. Mrs. Joan Cassell heard a plea on the radio that night for extra blood donors. On the following day, Monday 24th January, at Lewis's in Birmingham, shortly afterwards she and her sister began as donors for a long time.

Mr. Loveridge on duty that evening at Summerfield Hospital Heard an appeal on the 6.00p.m. B.B.C. News for off-duty nurses and theatre staff to go to the General and Accident Hospitals to assist with crash injured. It was over the radio on the Sunday evening, that Roger Shenton learnt the train he had sent on it's way from Lichfield Trent Valley Junction box in the afternoon came to grief in Sutton Coldfield Station.

By late Sunday evening the more seriously injured had been sent on to Birmingham. Five had been detained at the Sutton Hospital.

Richard Shrive recalled "the crash was a major tragedy for the town and it seemed" to him "that everyone was very subdued and quiet for some time".

PRAYERS AT EVENSONG

David Gumbley was a member "of the choir at All Saints Parish Church, Four Oaks and it was during evensong that I noticed the vicar Rev. F. Keats prayed for the families of the victims of the rail crash, that was about 7.10p.m., I was unaware of the crash". After Church David persuaded his Dad to take him and a friend into Sutton. They looked over "the parapet at the mouth of the tunnel. A couple of coaches stood upright but the main part of the coaching stock lay askew at the platforms".

RAILWAY PERSPECTIVES

Saltley passed fireman, Ken Beasley, said "once the depot knew about the Sutton crash, he was one among a number of Saltley lads sent out on cycles to alert the 21A fitters at home, to sign on straight away". They were needed immediately to staff the Saltley Breakdown Train, being prepared to go to Sutton.

When signalman William Gilbert arrived late afternoon, once the Police confirmed he was a local signalman at that box, he was allowed on site and into the box. William had a steady flow of railway people who "all needed to use the phones". He saw that "tea and sandwiches were offered by the W.V.S. There was beer but none was taken in the box". From the signal box Mr. Gilbert could see the scene clearly. In his opinion the brightest lights on site were "from the Crystal palace Fair", loaned by the Pat Collins organisation.

CHAIRMAN'S SALOON

Passenger shunter Dennis Gaule was on night turn on 23rd January at New Street Station. He was instructed to keep the "through siding clear for Sir. Brian Robertson's private saloon", where it was to be stabled after arriving from Cheltenham, his home station at the time. The Chairman of the British Transport Commission, seems to have changed his plans. Dennis commented, "he was not seen. I understand he travelled in the saloon further up the Sutton line, which was stabled in the Erdington area".

NOT ON ANOTHER TRAIN

Mr. Langthorne and his girl friend went with quite a lot of passengers down to the Congregational Church hall in Station Street, where they had refreshments. "We stood about talking, some people were dazed", Mr. Langthorne commented. Most were debating what their next moves would be, for him and his girl friend, "how could they get to Worcester?"

A railway official arrived to instruct them to catch the halted Bristol - York train back to New Street. Mr. Langthorne was "indifferent" about going on an express that nearly made it a double tragedy. His girl friend was very nervous being very reluctant to climb the ladder on to the train, to be drawn back to Birmingham. A special train left for the West Country, after refreshments, from New Street at 7.32p.m. for the uninjured passengers. Work carried on throughout the night. Fresh crews of the various services began to take over next morning, with an unexpected railway innovation for passengers without a train service to New Street for two days.

FOOD FLYING SQUAD

The Sutton Coldfield Food Flying Squad, a Civil Defence organisation, manned by the W.V.S., was set up on a Sutton station platform from 6.30p.m. on the Sunday until 10.30a.m. on Monday 24th. The food had been provided by Sutton shop keepers, until supplies arrived from railway authorities. The four W.V.S. Staff worked the sixteen hours. The squad had a convoy of eight vehicles, available to go anywhere in an emergency, the News noted. The organisation appealed to women who could cook and drive to join it's appreciated volunteer force.

LATE NIGHT DOORBELL CALL

Aston engine driver Ted 'Buttons' Higgs remembered it was "just 10.20p.m. When the doorbell rang. There was Geoff Butler on the step with a written request to book on immediately for driving duties as there had been a bad smash" that afternoon "at Sutton Coldfield". Ted was sent with engine driver Eric Morris and two fireman to

Sutton in the Bushbury Shed road van. The police stopped the van when they arrived at the scene, but let them through. Looking down from the footbridge windows on the upside "it was like looking at a newsreel at the cinema". Having walked up to the front of the train "its coaches all leaned over towards the down (Lichfield side) platform. Ted noticed that all the "carriage bogies had left the bottom of the coaches and were bunched up together, one behind the other". It was about eight hours after the crash, some time after midnight and "all the passengers had long since been removed". The Bescot crane was at work on the carriages at the north end of the scene. The engine 45274 was at the end

Jim Weston at the Four Oaks and Erdington instruments in the Sutton box. Mr. Weston had a call at home to go to the box and give assistance as required with the crash situation. (Dave Weston collection)

of the down platform standing upside down, its wheels pointing to the skies". The Saltley breakdown crane was on the smokebox end of the loco. The Rugby crane was in the bay platform, which had been dug out to accommodate its stabilisers. The two cranes were working to get the engine on its side.

PAINTLESS

Inspectors Allen and Harris sent Ted and his mate to relieve the men on the engine on the Saltley breakdown van. Ted and his fireman made the freight locomotive safe, then went to see how the work was progressing in the early hours of Monday 24th January. Ted noted, "The tender had been lifted off its side and put onto the bay platform track. Its right side had been dragged along in the derailment so that all the paint had gone and it was bright metal. The three axle box covers had gone and the axle ends were also bright metal. The cranes now had 45274 on her side with the right side uppermost".

DRIVER AND FIREMAN'S RESTING PLACE

A doctor went up a ladder to the deceased train crew in the cab roof which was folded around them. With the doctor back on the ground, the carriage steam heater pipes off the back of the loco's boiler were cut to release the fireman's arm. During the doctor's next visit up the ladder he carefully removed "all the things from the pockets of both men" and fully released the fireman.

The fireman's body was subsequently placed in one of the station's upside waiting rooms, used as a temporary mortuary. The driver's body was recovered and placed on a stretcher. "As the stretcher party went down the end of the platform, the men stumbled and fell over some debris. The driver's body fell off". Having been carefully replaced on the stretcher, the body was also taken to the mortuary. After that crucial series of movements had been completed "the breakdown crews stopped for a rest and some food".

W.V.S. CANTEEN

Another upside (Birmingham) waiting room was "being used by the local W.V.S. as a Canteen for all the various people working at the scene and the food came from the Queen's Hotel at New Street, Birmingham". After initially declining food, Eric accepted and enjoyed a bacon sandwich. Local Fire Brigade firemen kept the locos topped up with water.

At some point during the previous night, special saloon, M 45000 was attached to the rear of a Euston - Wolverhampton train to convey the Chief Motive Power Superintendent to the crash. The vehicle "was then worked to Sutton from New Street and put into the goods yard".

It's strange how "silly little things get remembered years later", Ted wrote down of the terrible incident. Ted noted "that Eric's fireman was wearing thick crepe-soled shoes and sat too long with his feet resting on something very hot on the footplate. The soles melted". Ted "was relieved after ten hours on duty and felt more tired than if I had been firing all night. It was such a harrowing experience I was glad to get home". Driver. M.C. Parker dragged "45274 to Aston in broad daylight, minus her front bogey which was taken to Crewe from Sutton".

MONDAY MORNING RELIEF
Similar to driver Higgs guard G.R. Bibb from Bescot, was called to assist at the crash. Guard Bibb however, was detailed on Monday morning to go by minibus to the crash site, working "to the orders of inspectors there". He recalled, "one crane was working from the rear into the wreckage, another crane was working from the front". Sixteen hours after the derailment he saw, "the loco was buried into the platform". Even later in the afternoon, "what was left of the boiler and firebox were still hot". The goods guard complimented the W.V.S. They did a "grand job of work in supplying food and drinks, even cigarettes etc".

LATE AFTERNOON START
David Gumbley and two other B.V.G.S. Boys went to the scene in their Monday dinner hour. "They looked through on the Birmingham side railings near the water crane. The twisted metal and sheer destruction was appalling. The front coach was leaning almost upright, against the platform edge but the engine was on it's side on the opposite platform. "We were late back to school but for a reason I never worked out, we were just waved to our places and not questioned. Mr. Crook the Physics teacher was a kindly man. Others would not have acted so sympathetically".

THIRTY YEAR RE-OPENING
Local newspapers reported bus services would be strengthened into the City, catering for the large number of railway commuters but nothing about the re-opening of a railway station for travellers preferring trains to buses even after the train crash the day before.

Bill Alcock, retired Saltley engine driver informed me, "We lived at Aldridge at the time of the Sutton Coldfield disaster. On the Monday morning I travelled to work at Saltley on the first train from Aldridge (about 7a.m.)". To his amazement the train stopped "at the old Sutton Town station and passengers got on". By Tuesday 25th January he had another surprise. "I was on an earlier turn of duty and we took empty stock from Saltley carriage sidings to Sutton Park and then worked a train (about

7.45a.m.) to New Street, stopping at Sutton Town, Penns, etc." The two staggered station buildings of the Town's Midland Railway station seen from the Midland Drive frontage are clearly identifiable in the 1950 Simmons Aerofilms photograph, on page 117 of Sutton Coldfield in the forties, Brewin Books, 2003. Details of the Town station closure and petition by 566 persons, is outlined in Sutton Town, the forgotten station pp 58-60, Cross City Connections, Brewin Books, 1990. The station officially closed on 1st January 1925, to be re-opened for those two days in January 1955.

The Walsall side of Sutton Town Station in Midland Drive opened in 1879 and closed in 1925, but re-opened for two days, 24th and 25th January 1955. (Mike Lewis)

SINGLE LINE WORKING

David Wiseman wrote about the railway operations during the line's close down to passenger traffic and freight services between Sunday afternoon and Wednesday morning. "Single line working was introduced between Erdington signal box and Sutton Coldfield signal box to enable railway cranes and wagons to be used for relaying the damaged track and platforms". Mr. Wiseman referred to the "bus services replacing the steam trains of the time". He became involved in an administrative role with the crash after effects. The disposal of the personal belongings of the people involved in the crash, were brought to the offices of the Divisional Passenger Manager, located in the Queens Hotel at New Street Station. As a member of the D.P.M.'s personal staff the belongings were dealt with by David when the claimants called.

NEWSPAPER COVERAGE

A man on his day off in Lancashire was reading the Monday morning newspaper in bed. Mr. Lloyd informed me he read the head lines stating "a family who had been to a wedding had been involved in the train crash in Sutton Coldfield, the afternoon before". To his distress members of his family were named. Apparently a telegram had been sent to him but had not been received. His younger sister, nephew and niece had all died. Four other family members were in hospital. It was about tea time when he reached Sutton Coldfield on the 24th. "His father was in a single ward, having been knocked out and received a bad gravel rash and cut tendons". His sister

Margaret was also in a single ward with a fractured skull and badly cut and bruised. His brother-in-law, Raymond, was able to walk about. He had bruises and was in shock. His nephew, David, was in a children's ward with a fractured pelvis.

News reporter, John Wood, in the next few days "pieced together stories of local people. A boy's picture of the doomed train, taken only minutes before the crash, appeared in the Sutton News and later in many national newspapers".

SIX YEAR OLD IN GOOD HOPE

David wrote to me. His own personal memories, being only six years old at the time, are minimal but quite vivid. "I do however particularly recall six weeks in Good Hope hospital and whilst I didn't really understand the reasons why, I was aware of great kindness, lots of gifts, lovely nurses and visits from the Police". Another strong impression upon him was "the visit of the C.I.D.", to his bedside.

Mr. Harrison explained, at the time of the accident the family lived in Bloxwich. After the accident they moved back to his mother's Herefordshire village, "where she continued to tend 'her' churchyard plot with tender loving care".

Back at the Kent R.E. Camp, I read the national papers like Mr. Lloyd, with almost disbelief, showing views of Sutton Coldfield I knew well, yet in a few days,

With debris still around the Sutton Coldfield L.N.W.R. Station, the route was re-opened with the 6.10a.m. from Four Oaks. Mr. Shallis approaches the foot crossing at Sutton. (John Hicks)

the media left the town and survivors to work things out themselves. The national papers had new topics to deal with.

Before the re-opening, Julie Bishop's policeman boy friend walked around the site with her. She commented "it was deathly quiet. I still have an image of desolation". The visit was probably on Tuesday 25th January. "There was no one else about", she recalled.

LINE CLEARED

The 1884 L.N.W.R. Sutton extension route was sufficiently cleared to re-open to passenger and freight traffic on Wednesday 26th January. The John Hicks picture makes it clear, work carried on, with rubble and stock still around. Four Oaks Station Master John Shallis, probably just alighted from the Burton service, is on his way to cross the line.

The locomotive in the photograph, 40633 was a 17B shed engine, probably diagrammed on the Burton - Lichfield, Sutton Coldfield - Birmingham New Street train. This particular engine was known to driver Allen and the passenger service.

INQUEST IDENTIFICATION

In Sutton Coldfield magistrates court on 26th January, H.M. Coroner C.W. Iliffe Esq., conducted the inquest with a jury. After evidence of identification and cause of the death of the seventeen deceased persons, the Coroner adjourned the inquest.

COACH AND LOCOMOTIVE STORAGE

Being away on National Service I was not sure what happened to the stock and loco after the mishap. Rob Jones recounted coaches from the Sutton crash were "removed and stored in the up-side sidings at Four Oaks", that I knew well. The stock was probably photographed by enthusiasts and the media.

Ted 'Buttons' Higgs, an Aston shed driver and keen photographer, who took notes on his Sunday night - Monday morning duty at the crash site, took two photographs of the 'dragged' heavily damaged locomotive, 45274, during its temporary storage at Aston (3D) motive power depot. Ted's two

This rare picture of the mangled footplate of 45274 at Aston Motive Power Depot, awaiting transfer to Crewe, shows the limited chances, conductor driver Allen and fireman Howell had to survive the crash. (Mrs. M. Higgs collection)

Driver Higgs side view of 45274, reveals the heavy impact on the cab and footplate. (Mrs. M. Higgs collection)

rare copyright pictures, loaned by his widow, reveals and indicates the limited chances conductor-driver Allen and fireman Howell had of survival, from the state of their engine.

BURTON FAREWELL

Driver Allen's relative spoke of the railwayman's funeral and burial on Thursday 27th January in Burton on Trent. It was a very difficult event for the family. There was a large Congregation to say farewell to the well liked and respected long term Hawkins Lane driver, including a large presence of Horninglow railway men. Many wondered how such a keen dedicated, experienced driver could be involved in such an accident. Was there critical significance in the unheeded hooter? Mr. Allen was buried in the same grave with his young son. A relative in a railway journal in 2003, wrote 'Mrs. Allen had no pension or money from the railway'.

SILENT VILLAGE

A contributor wrote that in the mid 1980s he was looking at headstones in a Midland village churchyard. His attention was attracted to the name "Sutton Coldfield", referring to the 1955 train crash. He had located the graves of the family members spoken about by Mr. G.E. Lloyd. A member of Bishop John's clergy sent in the picture taken of the village location. Mr. Lloyd's "most vivid memory of the funerals was that the shops in the village were closed", as the community's identification with the intense pain of losing loved ones in the Sutton train crash. A further recollection on that sad day, "was a policeman on point duty, the first I had ever seen in the village". The 'Citizen' reporter noted, "The tragedy has deeply shocked the whole village". The families, Mr. Lloyd shared, "moved back to the County, because my father was on his own and badly affected with the smash". His wife had died thirteen months before. Both the County and Burton families found it difficult to talk about the accident, though in later years the issues were considered more readily.

The memorial to John, 8 years and sister Jean, 5 years, who with their mother did not survive the Sutton train crash. (Mike Gasper)

TEST RUNS

To assist in answering some questions about the 23rd January railway accident, two train test runs were held on 31st January and 24th May, simulating the same situation, with locomotive and stock of similar age and condition as 45274 and ten coaches. Lieutenant-Colonel G.R.S. Wilson mentions in his official report on the accident that the 31st January test run, if continued unchecked would have resulted in the train running "at least at 61m.p.h. at the foot of the gradient at the Sutton tunnel entrance". It was further predicted the rising gradient through the 171 yard tunnel would have reduced Driver Allen's train to at least 57m.p.h. at the time of the derailment in Sutton station. The 24th May test run recorded the simulated 23rd January train reaching 52½ m.p.h. through Four Oaks station, after steam had been shut off at the entrance to the station.

The Chief Inspector emphasised the crash could have been prevented or the consequences seriously reduced if Guard Harrison had the "courage of his first conviction to make the full brake application".

It was brought out in the inquiry, that it was difficult to explain "this extraordinary lapse on the part of a driver with such a long record of trustworthy service and who had an intimate knowledge of all the characteristics of the route".

Apparently Driver Allen had not driven a diverted passenger train that way for some while. It was pointed out that a normal three non-corridor stock passenger train on the Sutton line would require stopping at each station, so speed should be considerably lower on approaching Sutton tunnel and it's sharp curves.

WARNING NEEDED
The Chief Inspector reflected that Driver Allen was trying to keep to the tight 15 minute Lichfield T.V. - Sutton Coldfield booking and had not driven that way for six months. He wondered if the Horninglow driver "may have forgotten the 30m.p.h. restriction through Sutton Coldfield tunnel". In the opinion of Lt. Colonel G.R.S. Wilson, "there was a need for speed restriction signs to advise, warn and remind drivers".

FURTHER CONTRIBUTIONS
Trade Union Official Mr. J. Brown was aware 45274 was "a notorious rough rider", with many drivers reporting the engine because of those poor riding qualities. But it had been examined on Saturday 22nd January and it was "found that there was nothing wrong with it".

Mr. E. Nunnery, the Permanent Way Inspector said there was a 40m.p.h. speed restriction on this stretch of the line between "Four Oaks to Sutton platform, then 30m.p.h through the station". The restrictions had been imposed because of the severity of the curve through the station and because of the hill gradient from Four Oaks to Sutton Coldfield.

Through the Sutton Coldfield News, the extended Lloyd family named as the 'hardest hit family' expressed their gratitude to the doctors, matron and staff at Sutton Coldfield Hospital and many unknown friends for their kindness, help and sympathy in a triple bereavement and for the floral tributes.

TINTING EXPERT IN TOWN
Gradually Suttonians began to show interest in subjects other than those mainly concerned with the train crash. Yet news items would from time-to-time take them back to 23rd January. Anne Scott on the High Street, Sutton, brought in a hair tinting expert for two days to give advice and answer any problems, "you may have in regard to coloration, brightening, glinting etc.". It was assumed men would not be attracted to such hair treatments.

STREETLY BECOMING A SLUM?
Three members of Aldridge Urban District Council heard complaints about, a) bad roads, b) poor street lighting, c) inadequate school accommodation and d) the building of factories in the area by the County Primary School Parent & Teachers

Association. The clerk to the Aldridge U.D.C. heard, "Streetly may become a slum if more factories are permitted". At the time there were factories producing plastics, wood worked products and other smaller ones in one part of the district.

The P.T.A. representatives reminded the Councillors further factories will come within the residential area. Assurances were made, "No more factories will be built", the clerk stressed. The County Planning Officers had thought it proper to have a small industrial area near One Hundred Acre Wood.

AUSTRALIA BECKONS
Suttonians and other West Midland residents were invited to "live your life in sunny Australia", employed as Tram and Bus conductors earning £12-£18 for a five day week of 40 hours. Overtime available. The Melbourne company needed 500 additional staff. Successful candidates within the age ranges, single men 19-40, single women 21-30, would be nominated for assisted £10 passages. Applicants would be interviewed in the West Midlands by Melbourne Transport Board personnel.

CHICAGO INTEREST
A local reader of the News, sent in the front page of the Chicago Daily Tribune on January 24th. It had a two-thirds of a column on the rail crash. The 'lady in blue jeans' was mentioned. The scale of the map 'made Sutton Coldfield about 30 miles from Birmingham'.

Three members of Sutton Coldfield St. John's Ambulance Brigade were presented with Meritorious Service Certificates for outstanding services and devotion to duty at the disaster. The awards went to: Divisional Officer A.V. Hunt and Privates A. C. Dayman and F. Titmus.

INQUEST VERDICT
The Sutton News of 25th February informed readers an Inquest on the train crash had closed earlier that week, when an all male jury returned a verdict of "Accidental death on the seventeen victims", agreeing the accident was due to "Excessive speed". The jury foreman told the Coroner, Mr. C.W. Illife, "We think a contributory cause was the knocking (in the engine), which would distract the driver and not allow him to make the usual estimate of speed".

Summing up, Mr. Illife said "the consensus of opinion was that the train was travelling faster than 30 m.p.h. and that it fouled the rails as it left the tunnel and took the curve through the station".

Mr. Illife continued, "I do think it looks as if there was an error of judgement on the part of the pilot driver. Had he been alive I don't think you would have considered the question of criminal negligence and manslaughter", he told the jury.

Chapter Six

ADJUSTING TO TRAGEDY

INVALUABLE RADIOS

At the opening of the new ambulance depot in Boldmere Road, Ald. B.H. Hunt commented, "I don't know what we would have done without it in the January 1955 Rail disaster," referring to the 1954 installation of radios in Warwickshire County Council ambulances. In the 1954/55 operating year "costs of £3,000 had been recovered and a figure almost as big had been saved". In the same building a new clinic was opened, that had been waited for "a long time". The County Medical Officer, Dr. S.W. Savage informed guests at the new clinic, "Life expectancy of a baby born in 1840 was 41 years, in 1943 it had risen to 70 years". Nuclear materials are to help "in medical practice".

FIRST STEAM TRACTOR IN THE DISTRICT

It was claimed, Mr. and Mrs. W. Salt of Slade Road, Roughley, may have been Britain's longest married couple of 69 years, spending the anniversary quietly in their Roughley home. From the time Mr. Salt was 10 years old until he retired at 65, he worked on the Canwell Estate. His employment included driving the first steam tractor in the district hauling ploughing equipment.

INCLUSIVE AIR TRAVEL

The two Tudor Travel Bureau Ltd. Offices at Beeches Walk and in Erdington, promoted an eight day inclusive air travel holiday to Rapallo on the Italian Riviera for 45½ guineas. For a similar price the local company offered an eight day air travel holiday to Innsbruck with excursions to Salzburg, the Dolomites etc.

UGLY HOSPITAL BUILDING

Residents living in twenty Rectory Road houses, were shocked and angry about "the unsightliness of the hospital buildings being constructed opposite their homes". There were six single storey wards, with inter-connecting passages and red painted corrugated iron roofs. The Chair of the Sutton Coldfield Town planning committee said, "We had no say at all. They came and started building without permission, because they didn't need it".

Some residents described the hospital buildings as "Army barracks", or "a Prison", none thought it looked like a hospital. Workman had been at the site for about three years and "the work is progressing terribly slowly", one housewife commented. Following local protests and 1953 petition the hospital chimney stack near the road was re-sited at the back of the building, though it remained a nuisance. Smoke poured from it all day and residents were afraid "of it's effect on their health". Suttonians wanted a modern hospital but Good Hope was not measuring up to their images.

'CONGS' HELP RECOGNISED

The Park Road Congregational Church magazine reproduced a letter to the Church secretary, Mr. W. Parsons, from the County's Chief Constable Mr. G.C. White. He wrote "I am writing to thank you for the facilities provided in your schoolroom for the feeding and checking of passengers immediately following the serious railway accident". Mr. and Mrs. Grainger were singled out "for the assistance they gave". Many other unnamed 'Cong' helpers were also appreciated by the County Constabulary.

TRAIN CRASH INQUIRY RESUMED

63 year old Gloucester driver, Mr. J. Martin, had recovered from the accident, so the inquiry was resumed to hear his evidence. Amongst other issues, Col. Wilson, Chief Inspector of Railways, read the rule relating to conductor drivers which said "the train driver must study the speed restrictions for the part of the line over which he was conducted". The driver advised the Inquiry it would take him a "long time to learn the route". He reminded the Chief Inspector that he was "a main-line driver not a diversional driver". Driver Martin, responding to the C.I.'s question, "Did you gain the impression that the engine was unsafe?" He replied, "no, just uncomfortable". The Gloucester man thought when driver Allen "took over the train it was driven a little harder than he would have done".

Col. Wilson said the fact that Mr. Martin was in one of the coaches saved his life. The driver replied, "That is what you call fate". Years after, a West Midland train crewman informed he had seen Mr. Martin at the man's home depot, carrying out duties at the shed.

GULLS SUTTON STOP-OVER

"Gulls" the News noted, "were often seen flying over the town", but a strong wind from the east coast, blowing all day, saw the birds settling down for a breather on the Coppice View Road School football pitch. George Frederick Road ornithologist Mr. F. Oldridge, thought there were "about 50 gulls".

SUTTON PARK WINDSCREEN BADGES

On production of their vehicle log book or driving licence, Sutton Coldfield motorists were able to obtain a Sutton Park windscreen badge from the Main Gate, Boldmere,

Banners Gate or Streetly entrances in March 1955. There was no compulsion to have one, "but it will make it easier for our Parkmen to see who are residents and who are not", the Chair of the Parks and Estates Committee told the Sutton News. It would avoid local residents having to pay an entrance fee into Sutton Park.

SALARY INCREASES

Sutton Coldfield Town Council agreed to salary increases for three head of departments. The Borough Treasurer increased to £1,622. p.a; the Borough Surveyor to £1,932. p.a; with the highest paid being the Town Clerk at £2,042. p.a.

SUTTON FIREMEN AT HALFORDS

Two crews of four fireman from the Sutton Fire Station helped fight the £3 million blaze at Halfords Ltd in Birmingham, across the road from the City's main Fire Station. Sutton's first crew left at 7.20a.m. with a pump escape, relieved at 9.00a.m. by another crew who remained at the scene for another three hours.

One fireman told the local newspaper, "the heat was terrific and it was not possible to get anywhere near the building". As the Sutton crew fought the fire, "All the scaffolding was falling and the walls were bulging". The intense heat of the fire was obvious as the water hitting the fire "just turned to steam and with that and the smoke it was impossible to see a thing".

A third Sutton crew and one from Coleshill went into Birmingham on standby duty. It may be recalled Sutton firemen had experience of a train crash near Tamworth, sometime before the Sutton crash. The Halfords fire maybe of use in Sutton in years to come.

COMMERCIAL TELEVISION

The Independent Television Authority (I.T.A.) had received planning permission for a transmission building at the Sutton Coldfield B.B.C. Television station site. It was the I.T.A.'s intention to "begin transmitting commercial programmes in the Midlands next December". Discussions about the joint use by the B.B.C. and I.T.A. of the B.B.C. mast were ongoing. If joint use was not resolved, the I.T.A. had located another four suitable sites on the north side of Birmingham.

It was anticipated most older T.V. sets could be converted to receiving commercial programmes. The conversions and new aerials were, "expected to be easy and cheap".

SERGEANT MAJOR'S VOLUNTEERS

Life as a National Serviceman had its occasional surprises as the request from the C.O. via the Sgt. Major, Sergeant and Corporal earlier related. Our Sergeant Major, at least to me, but I do not think I was on my own, was a formidable, threatening, intimidating tall regular soldier, who, radiated self-confidence in his appearance and authoritative instructions.

His authority and use of psychology was vividly displayed one weekday lunchtime. With four other sappers in the Hoo Camp, resting on our beds with dirty boots hanging over the bed end, we were regaining our strength after the morning's digging and filling holes. Wednesday afternoons were for recreation, so we felt we should benefit from an easier approach to whatever was offered.

The billet door was opened with a sense of urgency and in came the S.M., looking directly at each soldier in turn. His question got me shivering. "Any of you men enjoy sport?" It seemed an innocuous question, yet somehow I did not trust him. The four other sappers raised a hand immediately, I, in panic, lay still, arms firmly on the bed. The W.O. was pleased with the willing volunteers, asking them to report after lunch for a special sporting activity. The four went off, grateful to show their athletic prowess to the S.M. I questioned in my mind if I had wrongly thought ill of him! What sporting activities had I allowed to pass me by?

I cannot recall what activity was meted out to me that afternoon, but it certainly failed to excite or be a recreating force for me. How foolish I had been not to accept the S.M.'s generous chance to widen my knowledge and sporting skills! With reluctance I enquired of the four favoured sappers at tea, what fascinating athletic horizons they had conquered, through the S.M.'s Benevolence. To say my genuine question provoked a barrage of abuse and prolonged excessive swearing would be a serious understatement. Whatever sporting pursuits they took part in, they vented their anger vehemently on me. Perhaps they would admit my caution of not accepting the S.M.'s invitation at face value was to be commended. None of it!

After carrying out their recreational workout, they were accusing the Sergeant Major, at least in the non-N.C.O.'s mess, that he had conned and misled them that afternoon. The enjoyable sport they so enthusiastically volunteered for, was to pull the heavy roller over the whole cricket pitch, in teams of two, all afternoon. Although the four other sporting sappers could not admit I made the right decision, I knew for once, I had. My leg and arm muscles and back confirmed it, and so did theirs.

UNIT RESPONSIBILITY
Whether my fear energised decision not to volunteer to the S.M.'s con-trick became a talking point in the Sergeant's and Officer's messes, I do not know, but an order to be at the guard room one Spring Wednesday afternoon, in civvies, with writing pad and pen, made me apprehensive. Was the S.M. Getting his own back? Could this be a circuitous route to jankers?

The duty Sergeant advised me that I had been nominated for a privileged R.E. Unit responsibility. Surely they had the wrong sapper. I had failed my initial sapper training, having to take the lot again and still not gaining a pass mark. Yes, my sub-conscious advised me, the S.M. was taking the Michael out of me! Sergeant tested me on some simple multiplications. 5 x 6; 4 x 4; 5 x 1 + 6 ? Then a check on my long distance vision of two hundred yards away. I had to write down some numbers he called out to me. He was able to read the numbers I had written down correctly. It was a pleasant sunny afternoon and the covered military lorry had a collection of personnel I would never mix with, such as Corporals and Sergeants. On arrival at another R.E. unit, our team changed into cricket gear and I was taken to a chair near an empty score board. The team captain showed me a score card with our players' names and one with our opponents details.

Walmley C.C. 2nd XI at the Penns Lane ground, situated between Penns railway station and Penns Hall, on a chilly day. The teams' match umpire is on the extreme left of the back row. On the front row, second on the left is Captain Les 'Cap' Smith. The wicket keeper is Dick Clarridge. The author would have appreciated scorer Mrs. Gale's knowledge and expertise of cricket scoring when he was chosen as the Royal Engineer's Unit scorer with no prior experience for that appointment. (Alan Smith)

During the match, the umpires signalled to me with fingers and hand gestures that I did not understand. Fortunately the host team's scorer realised my ignorance and made me aware of byes, wides etc.

I cannot remember how we progressed, though the afternoon out had been enjoyable. With my writing gear I started walking back to our lorry, to await the team. The Captain called me back towards the pavilion, asking me to join the team and the host team. To my delight and surprise we had delicious eggs, chips, bread, butter, cakes with tea or coffee. They tasted like those cooked by mum. Apparently, even with my limited knowledge of cricket and scoring, I soon caught on, being appointed as the Unit's Official Cricket Scorer, travelling with the team to military venues in Kent.

Whoever nominated me for the position I was grateful to them. My enthusiasm for the job, probably ensured there would be no shortage of volunteers the next season, knowing the reward for accurate scoring was sumptuous teas at away fixtures.

ADAPTING TO ARTIFICIAL LIMBS

In the section 'Ian's true condition', his son Gary wrote that his father's injuries on the 23rd January resulted in the amputation of both legs and one finger. Ian was transferred from the Birmingham hospital "to a local hospital and convalescents nearer home". Gary remains proud of his father, "He came to terms with his disabilities in a very short time". On discharge from the R.A.F., Ian was offered "a job with British Rail, they said that due to the circumstances, he was promised a 'job for life'".

SIMILAR INJURIES TO DOUGLAS BADER

On recovering from his injuries, he was "fitted with artificial legs and had to learn to walk again". Ian went to the same hospital as Douglas Bader, both being in the R.A.F. and having similar injuries. "They wrote each other from time to time". Ian learned, "to cope with them", - the artificial legs - very quickly. He pushed himself as he always did". He had two very big incentives, "one - that he always said that 'he wasn't supposed to die in that crash, so he was grateful and was going to live life to the full'". The other incentive for Ian was to marry his childhood sweetheart. Gary described the other part of the second incentive, his father told everyone, that he "would walk down the isle on his wedding day, which exactly what he did only two years later".

PARK HOUSE HAPPY SOLUTION

The Friends of the Park Association informed the Council's Parks and Estates Committee that they congratulated them on resolving the difficult situation of preventing the park House "being taken over by interests outside the Borough". Ald. A.G.B. Owen had taken a lease on the property as a Café with living accommodation.

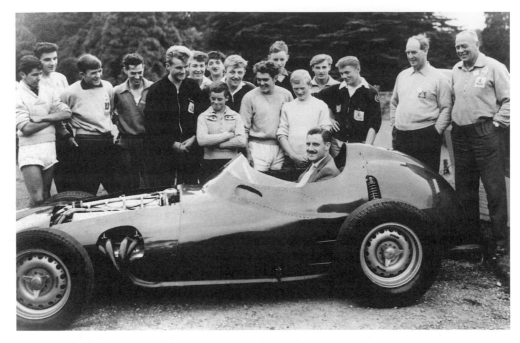

The Mayor, Ald. Alfred Owen had many interests. To prevent the Park House being owned by parties outside the Borough, he leased the property. This 1955 picture recorded the Mayor at a Boys Brigade Training camp with Graham Hill at the wheel of a new 2½ litre B.R.M. racing car, sponsored by Ald. Owen. On the far right of the photograph was B.B. secretary Major General D.J. Wilson - Haffenden C.B.E. (David Owen O.B.E.)

TEA BAGS AVAILABLE

The popular use of tea bags in the U.S.A. were on sale throughout Great Britain, with one bag providing three cups of tea. A 6/- packet supplied 200 cups of tea. The product was marketed as the only major change in tea-packing in generations. Since the tea bags introduction in G.B. a "considerable number of users" are beginning to buy them.

MINWORTH BULLIES

Three men, 2 at 24, one at 22 years were fined for assaulting and causing bodily harm to a seventeen year old youth waiting at Kingsbury Road bus stop.

Chief Inspector Croker advised the magistrates, "The men are well known in the village. When together, they are known as the village bullies, but when alone, typical of their type, they cause no trouble at all".

With the closure of the Falcon Lodge Farm, my father was employed at the Royal Naval Establishment in Minworth. He cycled there via Coles Lane, East View Road, Wylde Green Road, which was a gradient necessitating getting off and pushing the cycle towards Walmley village. (David Bassett)

APRIL 1955 HOUSES PRICES

A selection of properties from six Sutton Estate Agents in April 1955 reflect house prices at the time. £5,000 was the asking price by Shipway and Doble for a modern detached residence with four double bedrooms, two charming reception rooms, two secondary bedrooms on the second floor etc. With well secluded garden. Sorento was in Station Street.

A good family residence, with small greenhouse etc. and numerous fittings included in Eastern Road was £1,650 through Donald Luff, Powell & Co.

An attractive detached modern cottage style residence in Rectory Road with pleasant garden was available at £2,850, by H. Donald Dixon.

There was a two bedroomed property with a medium sized garden, near to Four Oaks station, shops and buses, for £1,650 in Jordan Road, by Slater Dann & Co.

Purchasers wanting close access to Sutton Park may have been interested in a well-designed two bedroom bungalow, with very latest American style kitchen, at £3,350, from F. Maitland Selwyn & Co.

An entirely labour saving type of accommodation in Bedford Road, described as a modern semi-detached, with easily maintained garden was available from Quantrill, Smith & Co, at £2,675.

Sutton Council tenants seeking a Council exchange enabling them to live in a quiet Staffordshire village, may have been tempted by an offer in the Sutton News. Tenants of a three bedroomed property in Shenstone wanted to exchange for a three or four bedroomed house in the Mere Green area of Sutton Coldfield.

INFANTS' SCHOOL TOO FULL
A school originally built for 90 pupils, according to the Sutton News, had more than 400 there in the Spring of 1955. With the "big extension of housing schemes for Walmley" the forecast was that the situation was "going to be increasingly worse". The Walmley Infants School was refusing at least 20 five year olds until September 1955 or January 1956. Some parents avoiding their children missing out in education had enrolled them in private schools. So limited was the on site school premises, some infants were being taught in the Parish Hall. The Divisional Education Officer anticipated the £40,000 new infants school would probably be finished, "before next winter".

PREMIERSHIP RETIREMENT
The News recorded that members of all political parties and of none in the local constituency would join them in wishing Sir Winston Churchill a happy retirement from the premiership.

LOMBARD PLACE
In the eyes of the News Editor, a miniature 'Lombard Place' had been created as Sutton's banking centre, close to Vesey Gardens. In close proximity, potential customers could choose from: Lloyds, Midland and Westminster Banks.

MYXOMATOSIS IN SUTTON PARK
Park Forester, Tom Allen, advised Suttonians that his staff had found "fourteen dead rabbits, killed by myxomatosis and some live ones obviously suffering". Mr. Allen thought the disease was likely to spread in the summer, carried by the rabbit flea. As rabbits caused a lot of nuisance in the small plantations of hardwood trees, such as oak and beech, the animals demise, "would probably be beneficial from the forestry point of view". The chairman of the Parks and Estates Committee gave the assurance "the disease was not dangerous to other animals".

B.R. RECOGNITION
Lord Rusholme, Chairman of the London Midland Region Area Board of British Rail made presentations to four people in recognition of their appreciated service to the community at the Sutton train crash. A silver tea service was made to Mr.

and Mrs. Norman of the Driffold and gold watches to Ticket Collector Arthur Attenborough of Lichfield and to locomotive Fireman Derek Smith of Derby.

PRESS SPECIAL

During a British Industrial Fair (B.I.F.) press special train, the Sutton Coldfield News Editor was assured, subject to delivery and staff training, the new diesel multiple units (D.M.Us) would be introduced on the Birmingham to Lichfield line in the early part of 1956. The local press representative was impressed by the D.M.U. used for the special train. He noted the "rapid, yet smooth acceleration and high speed running with a minimum of swaying. At 62 m.p.h one was able to walk the length of the train without seeking support". He found the compartments were well-lit with thermostatically controlled warm-air systems. The Editor complimented B.R. in finding a "solution to the problem of over-laden bus services and under-laden local railways". It was anticipated the D.M.U. Services would "be well run in by the 1957 World Scout Jamboree".

A May B.R. Advert promoted improved and intensified steam operated services between New Street and Sutton Coldfield and intermediate stations on weekdays. At a Sutton Town Council meeting, the improved steam train service was discussed. One councillor questioned why the services did not continue to Four Oaks, "where they were particularly needed in view of the vast housing developments of the district". The reasoning for not including Four Oaks would be requested by the Council.

DIESELIZATION COSTS

The News issue of 13th May reported on a British Rail Commission document that gave the cost of the complete dieselization of the Birmingham New Street - Erdington - Sutton Coldfield - Lichfield service at £350,000. The new funding promised a "much better service with an increase in train mileage of 66% provided".

OUT-PATIENT APPOINTMENTS

Some members of local women's organisations bitterly complained over the unjustified waiting occurring in out-patient clinics. Some patients turned up early or late for appointments to avoid long waits. Spokespersons understood, "the consultants were sometimes to blame, like the one who turned up for a 9.30a.m. consultation at 10.30a.m.". There was no explanation if the consultant had been rushed to an emergency, or if there were other genuine reasons for being late. A number of regular out-patients took sandwiches, should an appointment from mid-morning last into lunchtime or later.

SNOW MIRAGE
Freres was surprised by a deep need of Private Peter Jones, whose home was in the News catchment area. Peter was a member of the No. One Cold Storage Depot at Port Said. He had informed the columnist his, "main occupation was swimming". The Unit's open air facilities for swimming, "were five yards away, - the Suez Canal". Their other main pastime was football.

Private Jones "was hoping to get home a little earlier in 1956". He wanted to see some snow. Being in the heat at Port Said had made him aware, "how much I like the stuff".

PREJUDICE AT MERE GREEN
Some Mere Green housewives were dismayed by the prejudice a former German P.O.W., turned greengrocer, had received from local shopkeepers. Arthur married a local girl, who had lost her father during W.W.II. The Belwell Lane shopkeeper had lived in Sutton since 1951, but it was not until he, "opened the shop he was the victim of prejudice". Apparently, with the active support of housewives who recognised the consistently good service he gave, "I have more than trebled the turn-over", since he took over, he advised the local paper.

2,700 BABIES LATER
During the nine years Miss K.M. Scott worked at the Oakhurst Maternity Unit, 2,700 babies were delivered there, according to the Sutton News. Miss Scott joined as a Sister when the Unit opened with promotion to Matron in 1953. Miss Scott retired after 34 years in the nursing profession.

KEEP JAMBOREE SPENDING IN SUTTON
The local Chamber of Trade were co-operating with the 1957 Jamboree organisers in an attempt to keep as much trade from the world event within the Borough as they could. In particular they wanted to "prevent such items as catering orders going outside the town". It was anticipated suppliers throughout the country wanted to bid for such orders.

NATIONAL RAIL STRIKE
A national rail strike seriously hit the work load of the 100 staff at the Sutton Park Postal Customs and Excise depot, eventually bringing it to "a standstill." Superintendent Mr. T.A. Hook said, "Our normal routine has been thrown to the winds". Usually the staff handled between 1,000 and 2,000 bags of parcels each day, at the time they were only "dealing with parcels left from last week".

One shed with thousands of parcels containing goods for exports are awaiting transport, "and staff at the ports were not getting the post out". Normally the depot received two or three rail deliveries a day, with bags of parcels from the Middle East, Far East, Dominions, America, Europe and Eire. The Post Offices were not accepting parcels for Australia, New Zealand, India, Pakistan and Ceylon.

FORGOTTEN GLOVE TREATMENT

Erdington Housewives League Members were reminded how their treatment of nylon stockings had changed in the previous decade. Miss M. Yates from the British Royal Research Assoc., in London included the care of nylons in a talk on, "The care of fabrics".

"When nylon stockings first came out after the war, we treated them with delicate care", brought such memories back to the members minds. The thoughtful treatment included "putting them on wearing gloves". Nowadays Miss Yates pointed out, "we treat them not as a luxury but as common form of dress and handle them without any care at all". The speaker emphasised, "that frequent washing was beneficial to all clothing".

ASTRONOMICAL SOUNDINGS

Freres reported an increased interest in astronomy, stimulated by news of the receipt of radio waves from the stars. There had been "big strides in this practically new development in astronomy in America and Australia". In response to numerous requests and to foster the interest, a lecture had been arranged on 'Radio Astronomy', with the speaker from the University of Birmingham. The joint hosts were the Sutton Coldfield University Extension Society and the University's extra-mural department.

SIGNIFICANT IMAGE CHANGE

At the Mayor's service in the Park Road Congregational Church, the minister, Rev. T. J. Lander compared significant changes he had noted in the town between 1945 and 1955.

During the war years, the congregation were reminded "Hitler's armies were ranged against us, but the power of the nation was such that the threat was overcome, but since then, there has been a threat that something would happen that those armies could never achieve".

The minister pointed out, in his opinion, "there had been a breakdown of moral and spiritual life among the people". He commented on "the neglect of things such as common honesty". The chief need Mr. Lander considered to be necessary in Sutton was the development of a "community of people which was at it's very heart a religious community".

DAWN CHORUS

An article on the Sutton Coldfield Natural History Society's early morning visit to Sutton Park in June, may have whetted the appetite of some Suttonians to enjoy the first bird songs of the day. At 2.45a.m. there was a clear sky with a full moon. The first glimpses of green light were noted in the East and the air was warm and still, with no wind.

There was a distant whirr of a night-jar before the light was in the sky. Then a number of sounds could be heard. At 3.30a.m. a tawny owl, sixteen minutes later one robin sang, yet within a further four minutes a "chorus of robins was resounding from every point". Other birds joined in the full dawn chorus, such as blackbird, thrush, cuckoo, wood pigeon, chiff-chaff, willow-warbler and yellow hammer.

The light strengthened towards Bracebridge, where the "lovely, clear, rippling, song of the blackcap" was heard in several places. A redstart gave a "prolonged performance, enabling those not familiar with this song to get it by heart". About 35 birds were noted as seen or heard.

NINETY PER CENT DISAPPOINTMENT

A couple of weeks after a new chiropody service for old people in the town, operated by nine chiropodists, had been enthusiastically announced by Dr. J.R. Preston, at less than half the normal charge, the M.O.H. had to make another statement on foot care. With obvious disappointment he told the News 90% of the daily ten applications for the service "are going to be disappointed as many will not be eligible". Apparently the patients were those of "slender means and whose feet are sufficiently bad to keep them at home".

INFINITELY SUPERIOR LISTENING

40 music lovers and record collectors listened to the first demonstration in the district of High Fidelity tape recordings. During the interval in John Frost's showrooms on the Parade, a Hi-Fi authority said, what they had heard and later in the programme "was infinitely superior to anything he had heard before". He promised that the product was "a foretaste as to what one might expect" in the future.

UNAFFORDABLE LIVING

A Sutton Coldfield Institute of Further Education Course was run with working class folk in mind, amongst others, because soft furnishings were usually outside their restricted budgets. The experimental course that began four years before, eventually led to eight run in 1955.

Mrs. Aldridge the teacher, believed the course was "very popular because the cost of living is so high that many people cannot afford to buy the things we teach them to make".

The 110 Midland 'Red' service from Tamworth to Birmingham approaching Frost's show rooms where the new infinitely superior High Fidelity tape recordings were heard. (Birmingham Library Services)

DESERTING T.V. ?

Amongst the reasons to join the eight soft furnishings courses could have been a weariness with watching television. Stan Biley, Chairman of the Sutton Coldfield Old-Time Dance Club, founded by him and his wife in 1948, thought the growing demand for their weekly activity could be patrons "escaping from T.V.".

Stan told the News reporter "people were flocking to St. Peter's Hall, Maney, every Thursday". They were attracted by "genuine 'Old-time' with music by Vic. Moseley's King Nights of Gladness".

LANCASHIRE AIRING

A map-reading exercise by Wylde Green College Old Boys' and their wives or girl friends took them further than many similar events. Those who completed the route successfully arrived at Derby Airfield. As part of the Silver Jubilee outing, they were welcomed by fellow old boy Eric Lines a pilot captain with a Derby based airline.

To members and friends delight and with Mr. Lines' air hostess wife, the party were whisked off in a 36 seater Dakota aircraft to Blackpool. After spending an exciting evening in the Lancashire resort they returned home on the same route.

LOSS OF AN INSTITUTION

Owing to 'advancing years' the shop notice informed customers, Butcher Evans was closing in the summer of 1955. He had fed numerous kids with scraps of raw sausage meat as they clung to their mothers' skirts. Mr. Evans with his straw hat on a tilt tickled little ones under their chins. The butcher was one of many Suttonians' favourite links with their youth. One former raw sausage devourer informed the News, "There will be a great outbreak of nostalgia this week among readers of that proud little notice".

Evans and Roses were local shops that had served the community through the fat and thin years. (Birmingham Library Services)

FORTY SIX YEARS IN TEACHING

A few weeks before my eagerly awaited demob from National Service, it was likely the Royal Engineers in Kent, felt the same way, my former Victoria Road Boys' School Headmaster was retiring. Mr. J.H. Gregory of Tamworth Road, came to Sutton in 1919 from Dudley to Hill Boys' School as headmaster. In 1932 he was promoted to Head of Victoria Road Boys' School and he was my Headmaster from 1946 - 1949. Though it seemed much longer than that. He did not have a successor. Two schools were combined.

Mr. Gregory was presented with a cheque and his wife a basket of flowers by Geoffrey Gill, the head boy. Mr. J. Carter provided an album of photos, portraying various aspects of school life. Tributes were paid by Mr. J.K. Davis, deputy head at Banners Gate School, a former V.R.B.S. pupil, Mr. J. Fishwick, head of Minworth School, formerly an assistant master at Victoria Road and Mrs. W.E. Davis, a staff member when Mr. Gregory arrived in 1932. Praise was expressed for the headmaster's innovations including specialised teaching, school visits, the house system and the acquisition of a playing field. Regrettably I only recalled him for banging my ears with a clinched fist, when I misbehaved and not supporting my parents and me when a school bully broke my arm.

Other long term teaching staff retiring were: Miss S.E. Davies, Miss A.M. Alderson and Mr. H.L. Clinton, were also all spoken well of by the Sutton Coldfield Divisional Executive.

LOW COST ANGLIA
The well known Chambers of Sutton in South Parade advertised the new Ford Anglia, offering 'Five star motoring at the lowest cost'. The raved about vehicle cost £360 + £151: 2s: 6d P.T.A. total of £511:2s:6d.

JAMBOREE PREPARATIONS
Having survived the many hazards of two years as a National Serviceman, folk in the town had their minds thrown two years ahead to the World Scout Jamboree of 1957 in the 2,400 acre Sutton Park. The local populous were advised the initial preparations "are now well under way".

The main arena site had been cleared of stones by local scouts. It was anticipated there would be about six camping sites in the Park.

UNSUNG USHERETTE
Cinema patrons in the Chester Road Boldmere and Erdington areas found the Pavilion manager provided a local bonus act after the Friday and Saturday evening Organ music programme. At his encouragement a 24 year old usherette, changed out of her uniform, into an appropriate dress to sing a solo. The News item noted the "Solo went down well with the audiences".

TOO MUCH RELIGION
Parents of three Falcon Lodge boys voiced their concern about the "wicked practice of subjecting the lads to concentrated religion at a World Evangelisation Crusade camp, near Bridgnorth". Some of the parents visited the two week long W.E.C. Camp finding their sons attended services that lasted up to three and a half hours. There was encouragement for the boys to make a commitment to Christ, "with the option of pledging themselves to future missionary work". Mr. F. J. Wilday "thought the reports had been exaggerated but apologised. He had given an undertaking not to send any more children there:" Apparently other children from Falcon Lodge had gone in 1954 "and thoroughly enjoyed it".

The Sutton Coldfield News Editor added at the end of the article, "It cannot be too strongly emphasised that whatever the routine of the camp and whether it be good or inadvisable, it has nothing to do with the F.L. Mission Hall, which is doing excellent work in the neighbourhood".

CURATE'S DISAPPOINTMENT

Rev. David Locke, Acting Curate-in-Charge of St. Chad's, Whitehouse Common was disappointed he had no real discussion with anyone wanting to debate concern about the church, What it is for? and what should the church be doing in the local community? During his twelve hour plus sitting outside the Reddicap Post Office. He was pleased, however, to receive £60 towards improvements and repairs at St. Chad's.

WAITING ROOM DISQUIET

My British Railway employment after two years National Service, served in Worcestershire, Hampshire, Kent and Norfolk, resumed as an adult porter at the Sutton Coldfield, former London and North Western Railway station, in central Sutton, a ten minute walk from my Jerome Road home. In the mid 1950's the station had a regular, growing number of commuters to Birmingham in the morning, a considerable parcel traffic with lorries from Birmingham, delivering in and around the Borough. The extensive freight yard was well used for home fuels, cattle feed and the R.A.F. 216 M.U. at Whitehouse Common Camp.

My senior colleagues David Higham, John Forsythe, the Station Master and Tom Perks in charge of the goods department under the Station Master, soon recognised that I was not developing skills or confidence with a shunting pole. So whether I liked it or not lamping duties to all the semaphore signals and shunting equipment in our local area were mine on the one shift.

Similar to the previous junior porter duties at Four Oaks and adult porter work at Blake Street and Alrewas, station cleaning was of importance to the Station Master, therefore, to remain in employment, to the station staff. The horror of the station crash eight months previously was not a forbidden subject, though its being mentioned could arouse unease among staff and passengers. What I had not expected when carrying out cleaning in an upside to Birmingham Waiting Room was an unsettling eerie feeling connected with it being used as a temporary mortuary in the recent past. I think some other railway staff had such experiences.

Senior porter John Forsythe became a model for art students. (Sutton Coldfield Technical College)

OFFICIAL REPORT SUMMARY

The September 1955 summary of Lt. Col. Wilson's official report on the Sutton crash in the News, brought memories flooding back 'for thousands of Suttonians, wanted or not. The Inspectorate made a 'High Tribute' to local people and many were mentioned for their unselfish efforts and commitment to the rescue and care of the passengers and support of emergency service personnel. The first ambulance with the injured left the scene at 4.35p.m., 22 minutes after the crash occurred. The last injured passengers were removed from the wreckage by 7.10p.m. Col. Wilson found "that the track was well maintained". The derailment "was due to the complete disregard of the 30 m.p.h. speed restriction through Sutton Coldfield station". Criticism was made against the train driver, Mr. Martin who rode in the train and guard Harrison who did not have the courage of his convictions to fully apply the vacuum brake.

A frequent proposal by many later commentators on the accident was a recommendation by Col. Wilson, "that a more uniform procedure for defining clearly the position and degree of speed restrictions".

Alan Kirkham was advised that after the overhaul and running in of the crash engine No. 45274, one of its first duties was to be the "lead engine of two Black 5s on a Royal Train".

CRICKET RECORD

A well known name associated with local cricket was Mr. Bowerman. His 67 not out was a major factor in the Rectory Park team's seven wicket win over Burton. The visitors highest scorer was Illingworth with 64 runs. The Sutton 1st side had concluded the season on a succession of wins.

ESTIMATED 2 MILLION VISITORS

2 million visitors to the August 1957 World Scout Jamboree was predicted by Mr. R.H.T. Broad at a Sutton Chamber of Trade meeting, plus 33,000 scouts. Mr. Broad said "It would be one of the greatest events that had ever occurred in Sutton Coldfield". It was essential "that preparations start now!" The speaker referring to a possible royal visit, advised it was also "essential to see that the decorations in the town were second to none".

Perhaps, also in mind of the probable royal visit in less than two years, the B.B.C. TV. mast was having "its first face lift, since completion nearly six years ago". The new refreshing colour was 'battleship grey'". The mast had previously been unpainted. The paint work was to ensure that it was "not affected by corrosive substances carried through the air from industrial Birmingham".

Mr. R.H.T. Broad's idea of producing a pamphlet welcoming scouts at the World Jamboree in Canada, on behalf of the Sutton Coldfield Boy Scouts Association in cooperation with the Sutton Chamber of Trade, to the 1957 World Jamboree "were enthusiastically received in Canada". A further 3,000 in addition to the 7,000 distributed in Canada, were being sent "to Scout centres in many parts of the world".

Shortly after the hype by the Scouts, C. of Trade and the Sutton Coldfield News reporters, four letters in the paper gave readers doubts about the 1957 World event. Concerns included: i) unease about the continued deterioration of the Park. ii) not enough done since 1945 to bring about improvements, e.g. Insufficient planting of trees. iii) encroachment of holly on the older hardwoods. iv) almost total disappearance of fences around the woods. v) silting of pools. vi) failure to improve eye sores, such as the area below Keepers' Pool. vii) trouble due to insufficient money spent on forestry and general maintenance.

Lambretta Scooter 150 cc.
A favoured form of transport
for many Suttonians was the
Lambretta 150 Scooter, seen on
show in a local garden.
(Contributor)

Readers anticipated that damage caused during the few weeks of the World Jamboree, would be equal to normal damage over many years. Although it was anticipated the scouts would be careful, "we cannot expect the other visitors to be equally considerate". One contributor required that the cleaning and repair programme post Jamboree would need to be 'very thorough' and expected it to be expensive. Jamboree spokesman, General Lockhart thought that as the Jamboree would bring much money to Sutton Coldfield, a proportion of it should go to restoring the Park to its original condition. That investment should secure the Park's "natural beauty for the next 50 years". That would be 2007.

DOCTORS VIEW ON DUMMIES

In the News column 'A word with doctors' it was accepted doctors "had damned dummies with a fanatical fury". The two main reasons being i) sucking was thought to spoil the shape of a child's mouth, which gave the child a rabbity row of front teeth and ii) led to enlarged tonsils and adenoids. A further reason against dummies was that they got into unhygenic places.

The News adviser reported there were changing opinions in medical circles. Some doctors and psychiatrists could see no objection to young children having dummies. Some of those asked, felt the dummies aided happiness. Comforters, as they were called, "were in fact a good thing".

FOOTBALL CLUB'S MAJOR LOSS

One of the Borough's principle sports grounds in October 1955 suffered a major loss of a spectator facility. Sutton Town F.C.'s 80 feet long wooden grandstand was burnt down at the Coles Lane ground. The day following the fire an appeal was launched to raise £4,000 to build a new stand to accommodate nearly twice as many spectators in the same area. The Club President, Mr. Lewis said an old Army type hut would be put up at Coles Lane, providing temporary changing rooms. Players could also use the Supporters Club recreation room.

Nearby St. Michael's offered the Town F.C. "Use of their Boldmere playing pitch and changing facilities".

ZELDA AND ZORRO TO SUTTON

Sutton Coldfield had been chosen to have the first police dogs in Warwickshire. They were settling in, being trained in a light programme. Zelda (bitch) and Zorro (dog) were born five months before in Surrey. It was anticipated both dogs would be fully trained in the Summer of 1956 and available for tracking duties throughout the County. Their training programme was in the hands of Sutton Coldfield P.C.'s George Wilson and Derek Badham.

PHILHARMONIC SEASON OPENED

The 1955-56 season of the Sutton Coldfield Philharmonic opened at the Town Hall with a speech by Sir. Adrian Boult, who was present at the inception of the Society - 26 years before. He paid tribute to the Society and "the spirit which inspired them to foster music away from the central focus of the City".

The 47 members of the City of Birmingham Symphony Orchestra was led by Norris Stanley and conducted by Sir. Adrian. The main item of the evening was Vaughan Williams' Fifth Symphony, written in 1943. The reviewer commented the piece had been splendidly played and most economically by the conductor.

I think it was sometime in the fifties with my parents that we went to the Sutton Odeon, or perhaps it was the Town Hall, to attend a concert Sir. Adrian was conducting. We were very disappointed to learn it had been cancelled. I think it was our first trip to such a type of event.

DEATH OF WELL KNOWN MEDIC

A Medic that practised in Sutton Coldfield from 1899 until his retirement, soon after W.W.II, died in late October 1955. After leaving Cambridge, Dr. Thomas Betteridge was a house surgeon at Birmingham General Hospital, later living and working in Sutton. Many letters from former patients were received at his home, regretting his passing.

THINK BEFORE SPRAYING

A few words of caution by an Assistant County Horticultural Adviser were given to members of the Sutton Coldfield Gardeners Association. Miss Jensen informed her audience, "that it is now considered that many sprays do more harm than good because they kill both friend and foe alike, among the insects". She recommended reverting to old-fashioned non-poisonous sprays "such as Derris, for these are just as effective and far less dangerous".

FOR - AGAINST JAMBOREE CONTINUED

A woman News reader, in November, was "astonished and disgusted with the attitude of some groups of people, so concerned for the state of their beloved Park, when the World Jamboree takes place here". The correspondent was and still lives close to the 1929 World Jamboree site in Arrowe Park, Birkenhead. She advised Sutton News readers, "There was never any ill feeling between the town and the Jamboree Organisers. On the contrary, the scouts, on leaving, raised a beautiful memorial which stands in the Park today in recognition of the happy association".

Birkenhead remained proud to have been the site of the last Jamboree in England. "Come on Sutton", the lady concluded "welcome them - your Park won't be spoilt either".

SUTTON SETS AN EXAMPLE

Other local authorities, having checked out Sutton's scheme to borrow money from private investors, were following the Town's example. Councillor D.V. Smallwood, chair of the Finance Committee, thought "the putting up of the rate of interest, has got a lot to do with the way money has come in".

The Town Council found it was a good source of cheap money on a short term, which is what the authority wanted. The Government asked "that it be done wherever possible". The previous month's interest rate rose to 4¾% on a seven year loan and 5% on a ten year loan. Since then private investors loaned £20,000 to the Council.

Sutton developing at an alarming rate along the Birmingham - Sutton Coldfield - Four Oaks - Lichfield railway corridor. A Birmingham - Burton service between Four Oaks and Blake Street, with Sara Close houses under construction. (David Gumbley)

JAMBOREE BACKING FROM No.10
The Prime Minister, Sir. Anthony Eden promised Lord Rowallan, the Chief Scout, that "he would ask the Government Departments to give their fullest support to the 1957 World Scout Jamboree", in Sutton Park.

BEST KEPT STATION GARDEN
For the second year running Streetly Station won the Best Kept Station Garden Competition in the Birmingham District Area. The two porteresses, Mrs. E. Richardson and Mrs. M. Harvey of Aldridge, shared the work. Since 1951 they had won two 4th prizes, a first and a special in the annual contest. Also in the 1955 competition the station came second in the cleanliness and tidiness. Mrs. Richardson told the 'News' "It is our ambition to win that too".

COMMERCIAL T.V. SHORTLY
The Commercial T.V. Station was progressing well towards completion. The 450' self-supporting tower and programmes would be provided by Associated Television Ltd. On Monday - Fridays and Associated British Cinemas (Television) Ltd., on Saturdays and Sundays. The anticipated start was in February 1956.

Alternative to the small screen donated to the Sons of Rest, the members still found time to create their own entertainment. (Birmingham Library Services)

FALCON LODGE COMMUNITY HALL
There was much rejoicing on Saturday 17th December, when Lord Bennett of Edgbaston opened Falcon Lodge Estate Community Hall on the corner of Newdigate and Churchill Roads. Mr. H.J.Barber, chair of the Residents Association thanked Lord and Lady Bennett for their magnificent gift on behalf of the Estate.

Mr. Barber said "We had visions long ago of a hall but no chance of a grant for years hence. In fact it was a dream - may I thank Lord and Lady Bennett for making a dream come true".

After the 1955 Christmas Post, the Foreign Parcels Depot had dealt with more than 180,000 incoming parcels during the five days before Christmas. More than 160 temporary workers were called into work. It was reported that parcels were better packed. 1,000 parcels had to be repaired with 5,000 over Christmas 1954.

There were many homes in Sutton Coldfield over Christmas that had memories coming back to them of the tragic accident, eleven months before. There were other homes throughout the U.K. where Sutton Coldfield came forcefully back to them at Christmas, because there were seventeen individuals not there, to celebrate.

POST CRASH HARDSHIP
John Tidmarsh's Steam Railway article on the Sutton Coldfield crash, published in 2003, issue 280, brought a number of letters, including one from another extended family member from Burton-on-Trent. The man wrote about his perception of the lack of loyalty shown by the Railway towards the driver's widow. The contributor wrote that his "uncle Harold (Dick) Allen was a devout churchman who avoided Sunday working if at all possible, however, after completing his duties" at his Burton church, "he was met outside the church with a request to act as conductor driver on the 12.15p.m. York – Bristol express. Other drivers had turned down the working". A retired driver wrote to advise me, he was one of the driver's who declined that extra shift.

The nephew continued his letter, "Dick Allen was a fit, alert and conscientious servant to the company and the reasons why the train was travelling so fast in that section will never be known". The writer concluded his letter with the circumstances his aunt experienced, in those post accident days. Mrs. Allen "did not receive any pension of any kind and was put into hardship for the rest of her life". That first Christmas after the Sutton crash was a very difficult and traumatic one for so many.

PREVIOUS BOOKS BY THE AUTHOR

Cross City Connections: Brewin Books, 1990

This remains the book with the most data and pictures of the stations and railway lines in the Borough of Sutton Coldfield 1940-1990. A considerable number of contributors were railway personnel, and some of their contributions have now been 'borrowed', without permission, by later authors!

Wheels Around Sutton, Lichfield and Tamworth: Brewin Books, 1997

Against the background of the wider Midland 'Red', this book traces the living history of public transport in Sutton Coldfield 1913-1973, the emergence of A.T. Hastilow's 'Tudor Rose' Coaches, and Harper Bros of Heath Hayes. With previously unpublished material by staff and customers at Sutton Coldfield, Lichfield and Tamworth, this book provides new perspectives of public transport in these areas.

Sutton Coldfield in the Forties: Brewin Books, 2003

The first in a series, covering the Town's local history 1930s-1950 provided by many Suttonian's and temporary residents with more than 70 previously unpublished pictures. A unique insight into the life and lives of Sutton Coldfield during the inter-war years, through W.W.II, and the Town's adjustments in the early post-war era.

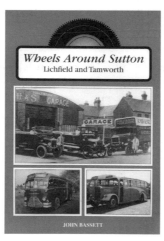
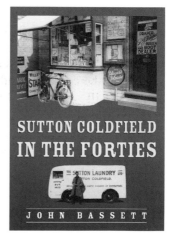

ABOUT THE AUTHOR

John Bassett was born, educated and lived in Sutton Coldfield from 1935-1963. His employment on British Railways 1950-53 and 1955-57 is covered in 'Cross City Connections'. In later years John qualified as a Field Social Worker, Further Education Teacher and Training Officer.

In 1984 he became a full time Railway Chaplain with the Railway Mission, becoming responsible in 1985 for the West Midlands, operating from Birmingham New Street Station.

After completing part-time courses at Northern College, Manchester and the University of Manchester over four years, John was ordained as a Non-Stipendiary Minister with the United Reformed Church in 1993. He was inducted on New Street Station with the encouragement and support of Railway management and staff.

At the request of Sir Richard Branson, the Rev John Bassett officiated at the renewal of marriage vows and promises by a Virgin Train Manager and his wife during a scheduled Wolverhampton to London Euston service. The couple celebrated their 25th Wedding Anniversary and the Train Manager's 25 years on the railways.

The Rev Bassett retired in 2000, with some of his time now being used to research his new series on Sutton Coldfield. He now lives in Lichfield.

The author, Rev John Bassett leading the 1994 D-Day Service for railway staff and customers on New Street Railway Station. (Railtrack/Caters photographic)